Persian Gran

No more "tenses", "articles", "pronouns", "irregular verbs", or "prepositions"! An innovative and long-overdue overhaul of the basic grammar of Persian, covering rules of pronunciation, categories of word, more advanced constructions, Persian script, and formal and spoken Persian, this book is ideal for beginners and especially those who have no background in languages or linguistics. It is written in a non-academic style, does not use complex terminology or irrelevant grammatical categories, and describes the grammar of a lesser-taught language in a straightforward and learner-focused manner.

Learn grammar the easiest, most efficient, and least time-consuming way possible with *Persian Grammar*.

David James Young is a lecturer in the School of Languages at Leeds Beckett University. With a deep interest in simplifying grammatical analysis, he believes strongly that language-learning materials should be accessible to *everyone*—not just those with a background in languages or linguistics.

Feedback, questions, and comments are welcome at
d.young@leedsbeckett.ac.uk.

Persian Grammar

David James Young

به نام خدا

for my mother

Contents

Also available in the same series:

Turkish Grammar

Urdu Grammar

Hindi Grammar

Spanish Grammar

Latin American Spanish Grammar

European Spanish Grammar

Brazilian Portuguese Grammar

European Portuguese Grammar

Introduction

This book is a grammar reference book. It teaches the basic, intermediate, and more advanced rules of Persian. However, it is not just a grammar book in the traditional sense; it also covers the pronunciation of Persian and Persian script, and it includes a list of several hundred common words in Persian. (Note that I do not use the term "Farsi" in this book; to me, using "Farsi" in English is like saying "I speak *le français*" instead of "I speak French".)

What is grammar?

Although this book covers both the pronunciation of Persian and Persian script and also includes a mini-dictionary, its main focus is *grammar*. Grammar is the set of rules of any given language. Traditionally, these rules are about two things: first, the types of words that exist in a language (what are more traditionally called "nouns", "verbs", "adjectives", etc) and second, how these different types of words appear together to form meaning. There are other rules in a language; for example, there are rules for pronunciation or for how the language is written, and modern linguists also use the term "grammar" to cover these types of rules. Given this book covers the pronunciation of Persian and Persian script, this is a book of grammar in the modern sense; it covers the rules you will need to produce and understand Persian.

Why is grammar important?

Grammar (in the traditional sense) is important because when learning any language, there is a clear difference between simply getting your meaning across and using the language with a degree of complexity and accuracy. If you learn the entire contents of a Persian dictionary, you would be able to say the Persian word for "multicultural" or "vice-president" or "hyperinflation" or any other less frequent word you can think of, but it is grammar that shows you how to put these words together into meaningful phrases. Admittedly, you could acquire a "basic knowledge" of French or Spanish for example by learning set expressions, as often occurs in modern language classes; yet, what this knowledge amounts to is often a collection of isolated phrases such as "How are you?", "I am fine, thank you", "Where is the beach?", "It is two o'clock", etc. With phrases like these, you may be able to go to France or Spain and have a limited conversation, but without some idea of grammar, you will never be able to understand why those phrases appear in the way they do or how to modify those phrases to say "Where is the supermarket?" instead of "Where is the beach?" or "No, I've had an awful day!" instead of "I am fine, thank you". At some point, all learners must learn at least some grammar.

Who is this book for?

Although this book was written for any learner of Persian, it was designed specifically with complete beginners in mind; it assumes no prior knowledge of Persian at all. Although learners who are already more advanced in Persian may find they know many of the rules in this book, these learners may nevertheless find the organisation and presentation of those rules different from what they are used to; hopefully, this will be a simpler and more elegant way of organising their grammatical knowledge. This book will be particularly useful for those learners who have not learned a language before or are unsure about traditional grammatical concepts and terminology (which are simply not used). Academically, this book is suitable for the undergraduate student embarking on a Middle Eastern Studies degree or the postgraduate student of politics or international relations learning Persian as an elective. Students of linguistics or languages may also find the way grammar is presented in this book different from what they are used to—again, hopefully in a positive and refreshing way. Primarily though, this book was written for learners with non-academic backgrounds and motivations: learners who are studying Persian informally in an evening class at their local college or learning at home with an audiobook in order to communicate with Persian friends and family.

What does this book do differently?

As mentioned earlier, this book does not use traditional grammatical terminology and categories. It does not use potentially confusing (and often completely unnecessary) labels like "noun", "pronoun", "relative clause", "adverb", etc. It presents a simple grammatical system of *objects*, *helpers*, *descriptors*, and *actions*—a system which can be used to classify all words in Persian. The rules governing each of these categories are discussed along with the rules governing how words of one category appear with words of another to impart meaning. The more complex structures of Persian are presented as *elevations*, which is a grammatical "tool" I have developed to describe more advanced structures in a language. In addition, this book differs from other grammar books in its approach to teaching Persian script; instead of the cumbersome four-way classification of letter forms ("initial", "medial", "final", and "isolated"), which is the traditional method of teaching the script, the script is taught through a simple *shape bank*; in my opinion, this is a more efficient way of learning the script and echoes how English speakers learn to write cursively. Finally, this book teaches the differences between "spoken" and "written" Persian. Again, unlike most other resources on Persian, the rules of spoken Persian are only described after the rules of written Persian. This is because the rules for written Persian are, in my opinion, more standardised and, being more uniform, are easier for the learner to acquire. It is then a much more straightforward process to consider the rules for spoken Persian simply as modifications that occur when speaking.

How should this book be used?

You should work through this book from Chapter One to Chapter Five slowly and methodically. Even if your knowledge of Persian is more advanced, there may be areas of grammar that need clarification for you, and as I mentioned, this book may present grammatical categories and structures in a way you have not encountered before. Do not use the index until you have worked through the whole book. The list of words in Chapter Three and the list of elevations in Chapter Four are presented only as a "springboard" for future learning; do continue to add to these lists. The overall aim of this book is that after completing it, you will have an efficient and simple "mental framework" that you can use to organise your continued learning. What this means is that after finishing this book, you should not need to consult additional formal textbooks.

What this book will not do is make you fluent in Persian—if your definition of fluency is being able to produce and understand Persian with very little effort. That is something that, in many ways, is entirely separate from knowing grammar; you might memorise all the rules, words, and elevations in this book (or any other book you can find on Persian), but you would still not be able to hold a natural conversation. This is because whereas grammar is knowledge, fluency is essentially a semi-physical skill; fluency requires that you put into practice all the rules you have learned, combined with all the words and elevations you have learned, while remembering to smile and be polite—all while remembering the backstory of the Persian soap opera you are discussing! That is something that takes practice. Finally, note that except for certain words that occur in some elevations that you do not need to translate, all the words used as examples in this book are included in Chapter Three.

Acknowledgements

Special thanks are owed to Emadedin Naraghi for checking the examples in the book and giving valuable feedback on the draft of the manuscript. His suggestions were very insightful and helpful, and any remaining mistakes in the examples or the analyses thereof remain my own.

Chapter One: Basic Rules

The rules in this chapter are the very basic rules of the language. The first section describes how to pronounce words in Persian, and the remaining four sections discuss the four categories I have used to classify all words in Persian: objects, helpers, descriptors, and actions.

Pronunciation

There are 28 sounds in Persian. In this book, these sounds are represented by the letters of the English alphabet. Partly because there are more sounds than there are letters to represent them, some sounds are represented by combinations of letters. The following letters represent sounds that are pronounced much the same as they are in English:

A	cat	*M*	man
Au	author	*N*	not
B	bat	*O*	hope
D	date	*P*	pass
E	hate	*S*	sad
F	far	*Sh*	show

G	**g**ate	T	**t**op
H	**h**at	U	f**oo**d
I	f**ee**t	V	**v**eer
J	**j**am	Y	**y**ellow
K	**c**alm	Z	**z**oo
L	**l**ook	Zh	vi**s**ion

These letters represent 24 of the 28 sounds of Persian I mentioned. The remaining four sounds need some explanation; these are sounds that are represented by letters that are not pronounced as they would be in English, and they are discussed in the following sections.

C, *Ch*, and *Kh*

The letter *C* is straightforward, though it is pronounced differently from English; it is pronounced as the CH of "chat". The letter combination *Ch* itself (together with *Kh*) is pronounced like the Liverpudlian pronunciation of K in "look" or the Scottish pronunciation of the CH in "loch". To make this sound, try saying the word "huge" or "human" but really emphasise the initial H sound. The back of your tongue should be raised up so that it almost touches the roof of your mouth. Alternatively, say a K sound as normal and try to feel where the two parts of your throat connect. You want to do exactly the same thing with your throat but stop short of connecting these two parts. This may sound difficult, but this sound is actually very common in many of the "European" languages you may be more familiar with from school or college. Although this sound may be difficult to pronounce at first, once mastered, you will probably find this a very natural sound to produce (in a way that you may never find the "rolled" R—see below).

Dt, Sz, Dz, and X

The letter combination *Dt* is pronounced as *T*; as an English speaker, you would probably pronounce this combination as something very similar to *T* anyway. Likewise, the letter combination *Sz* is pronounced as *S*. The letter combination *Dz* is pronounced as *Z*, as is the letter *X* (which also occurs in English words like "xenophobe" or "xylophone").

R

If you have a Welsh or Scottish accent when speaking English, the letter *R* will be simple to pronounce; the *R* in Persian is "rolled" or "trilled", much as it is in Italian and Spanish. If you have a problem rolling an R like this, try to say an L sound but instead of making contact with the ridge that lies just above your teeth, brush past that ridge very quickly with the tip of your tongue. This is a lot easier in some positions than others; for example, it is usually much easier to pronounce a rolled R before a vowel than at the end of a word or before another consonant. Remember that your tongue is like any other muscle—it responds to training; if you do find this sound difficult to produce, it will eventually get easier with practice.

Jh

The letter combination *Jh* is very simple; it is not pronounced at all! Some Persian speakers do "pronounce" this sound in some positions as a short pause or a closing up of the throat, but for our purposes, this letter combination can simply be ignored.

Q and *Gh*

Finally, the letter *Q* and the letter combination *Gh* are both used to represent a sound that is not used in English. It is probably best described as a form of gargle and is similar to the French or German pronunciation of R. To make this sound, say a G sound as you would in English but try to gargle at the same time. Alternatively, if you know French or German, say the R sound as you would in those languages but try to close up and then release the back of your throat as you do so. Like the sound represented by *Ch*, this sound does take some practice to produce comfortably; however, once mastered, you will wonder why you ever had difficulty producing it. As a general point about pronunciation, I would argue that as long as you can make yourself understood in Persian, you shouldn't worry so much if your accent is not perfectly "native". In fact, when interacting with native speakers of Persian, you may find that your imperfect accent is a great icebreaker.

Persian script

Persian is written in its own script, and this script is different from the one used in English. However, in this book, Persian script will not be discussed until Chapter Five, when the more complex rules of Persian are described. In my opinion, learning the script before you learn the basic grammatical rules of Persian ("grammatical" in the traditional sense of the word) or start to learn actual words and elevations is far more difficult than trying to learn rules, words, and elevations at the same time as you are trying to decode a completely new script. (It is for this reason that "informal" Persian is also not discussed until Chapter Five.) This is particularly the case with the script because Persian script does not usually represent all the sounds that occur in any given word; therefore, when you encounter a new word, you can never be completely sure how that word is pronounced. For example, you can open a dictionary of Persian, look up the word for "toothpaste", and find خمیر دندان; this is like finding "ChMYRDNDAuN". Unless you already know (as native speakers do) that "toothpaste" is "chamir-e-dandaun", the script will only ever allow you to make a precarious attempt at pronunciation.

Of course, a potential problem in leaving the script till later is that in Persian script (just as in English), the same sound may be represented by two or more different letters; for example, the Z sound in Persian can be represented by four different Persian letters: ذ, ض, ظ, and ز! Many grammar books of Persian simply represent these four different letters just as they sound: as a letter Z. This is a problem because when you subsequently come to learn Persian script and write words containing a Z sound, you will not know which of these four letters to use. Although I would argue that this does not justify the teaching of the script before anything else, I have bypassed this problem by using a system that encodes these spelling differences in the English letters used to represent Persian sounds; I have also used the letters of the English alphabet in a way that I feel looks natural and is intuitively easy to use. This means that when you do learn the script, you will know exactly how to both spell and pronounce every Persian word you have learned; this would not be the case if you encountered and recorded new words in Persian script. Of course, if you really do want to learn Persian script from the start, I have included a script version of all the example words and phrases given in this book. These examples will be useful to come back to and study if you learn the script at the later point I recommend.

Objects

As mentioned earlier, every word in Persian can be grouped into one of four categories: objects, helpers, descriptors, and actions. The system used in this book is different from traditional grammatical descriptions of languages (which use "nouns", "pronouns", "adverbs", "verbs", "adjectives", "articles", etc) because I do not want to describe an arbitrary division in any one of these categories where such a division would be (for Persian at least) completely unnecessary.   Compared to many other languages (including English), Persian has a very elegant and simple grammatical system.   Instead of making Persian fit either of the more traditional Latin or Arabic-based frameworks usually used to describe it, this book concentrates on teaching the rules of Persian in a way that is as efficient as possible.

Objects are one category of word in Persian. Objects are words that refer to things. They can be words for simple physical things like "book", "man", "cat", "city", "water", "planet", etc or more abstract things such as "anger", "intelligence", "love", "fear", etc. Words that are used to refer to other objects, such as words like "he", "she", "I", "him", "me", "us", "hers", "theirs", "ours", etc and names such as "David", "Tehran", "England", "Persia", "the Statue of Liberty", etc are also all objects. Finally, words that denote when something happened, such as "when?", "then", "never", "sometimes", words that denote where something happened, such as "where?", "there", "nowhere", "above", "out", and words that denote how something happened, such as "how?", "slowly", "definitely", "carefully", "well" are also all objects. Note that words like "never", "there", and "slowly" are simply "shortcuts" for larger phrases built around more concrete objects: "at no time", "in that place", "in a slow manner", etc. There is no need to introduce another category such as "adverbs", as other grammar books suggest.

Talking about more than one thing

As is often the case in Persian, there are relatively few rules to learn about objects. For example, unlike in many of the languages you may be familiar with from school or college, objects in Persian (as in English) are not divided into "feminine" or "masculine" groups as they are in French, Arabic, or Urdu for example; neither are there "cases" as in German, Polish, or Russian. In fact, the only rule you will need to learn that directly affects objects in Persian is how to talk about more than one thing. To do this, simply add "...*hau*" to any viable object, as follows:

کتاب

ketaub
book

کتابها

ketaubhau
books

Helpers

Helpers are words that give meaning to other words. The only thing you need to remember about any helper you encounter is where it goes and what it means. Let's look at an example; the helper "*yek*" in Persian appears before an object and denotes "a" or "an":

یک کتاب

yek *ketaub*
a book

یک مرد

yek *mard*
a man

No matter what other grammar books tell you, you do not need to worry about whether this word is an "article", "determiner", "preposition", "adjective", or anything else; all you ever need to learn about the helper "*yek*" is that it appears before an object and denotes "a". While we're discussing "*yek*", note that an object without this helper can denote both "book" and "the book" or "man" and "the man" etc; there is no specific helper in Persian that denotes "the":

کتاب

ketaub
book

کتاب

ketaub
the book

Other helpers also appear before objects, such as "*az*" – "from", "*be*" – "to", "*bau*" – "with", and "*in*" – "this":

از ایران

***az** Iraun*
from Iran

به شهر

***be** shahr*
to the city

با مرد

***bau** mard*
with the man

این کتاب

***in** ketaub*
this book

Just as in English, helpers can appear together:

در این خانه

***dar in** chaune*
in this house

با یک مرد

***bau yek** mard*
with a man

Helpers can also appear after objects; the helper *"pish"* denotes *"ago"* and appears after an object—as does *"bajhd"* – *"later"*:

یک ماه پیش

*yek mauh **pish***

a month ago

یک هفته بعد

*yek hafte **bajhd***

a week later

Helpers can even appear surrounding an object, like the helper *"ce ...i?"* – *"what ...?"*:

چه کتابی؟

ce ketaubi?

what book?

چه مردی؟

ce mardi?

what man?

Sometimes, a helper may have a specific meaning but not a specific location. Helpers like these include *"aure"* – *"yes"*, *"mersi"* – *"thank you"*, *"lottfann"* – *"please"*, and *"sóbhh be cheir"* – *"good morning"*, and they can appear pretty much anywhere. In this case, just use them as you would in English:

آره

aure

yes

مرسی

mersi

thank you

لطفاً

lottfann

please

صبح به خیر

sóbhh be cheir

good morning

The opposite may also be the case; a helper may have a specific location but not a specific meaning—at least, by itself. We have in fact already encountered a helper like this in the previous section: "...*hau*". If you remember, this helper appears attached onto the end of an object and denotes that there is more than one thing:

كتاب

ketaub

book

كتابها

*ketaub**hau***

books

Here, "...*hau*" does not have a meaning by itself; instead, it changes the meaning of the word to which it is attached.

The helper "-*e*-"

Another very important helper that does not have a meaning by itself is the helper "-*e*-". This helper appears between two objects and denotes that the first object belongs to the second:

كتاب مرد

*ketaub-**e**-mard*

the book of the man / the man's book

خانه ی زن

*chaune-**e**-zan*

the house of the woman / the woman's house

Now, take a look at the following objects:

او
u
he

او
u
she

آن
aun
it

آنها
aunhau
they

من
man
I

ما
mau
we

تو
tou
you ~one person

شما
shomau
you ~more than one person

When one of these objects appears with the helper "*-e-*", we can make a phrase like "his book", "my book", "our book", etc:

کتاب او
*ketaub-e-**u***
his book

کتاب او
*ketaub-e-**u***
her book

کتاب آن
*ketaub-e-**aun***
its book

کتاب آنها
*ketaub-e-**aunhau***
their book

كتاب من
*ketaub-e-**man***
my book

كتاب ما
*ketaub-e-**mau***
our book

كتاب تو
*ketaub-e-**tou***
your book

كتاب شما
*ketaub-e-**shomau***
your book

Note that these objects can also be translated as "him", "them", "me", "us", etc. If you find this confusing, this is actually the fault of English; in English, most of the words denoting "he", "she", "I", "we", etc have two forms: "he" and "him", "she" and "her", "they" and "them", "I" and "me", and "we" and "us". The situation in Persian is much simpler because the same form is always used:

با او
bau u
with **him**

از من
az man
from **me**

Finally, note that helpers do not just appear with objects; some helpers appear with words from the other categories discussed in the following sections—or even with whole phrases. Also, remember that when you are learning Persian (or any other language for that matter), you will likely encounter grammar books or other resources that divide helpers into a very wide variety of categories, such as "articles", "prepositions", "conjunctions", "interjections", etc. This is completely unnecessary; all you ever need to learn about any helper you encounter is where it goes and what it means.

Descriptors

Descriptors are words that describe objects. Words like "big", "small", "happy", "red", "yellow", "Iranian", etc are all descriptors. Words like "eating" and "eaten", "jumping" and "jumped", and "going" and "gone", etc are also descriptors, albeit slightly more complex ones. All these words are used to describe an object: "the big book", "the small dog", "the man is happy", "Iranian politics", "the apple is eaten", "the man is not going", etc.

Two types of phrase

Descriptors can appear in two types of phrase. The first type of phrase is "the big book", "the happy man", "red apples", "British people", etc, where the descriptor (in English at least) appears before an object. To form phrases like these in Persian, the descriptor actually appears after an object and is connected to that object with the helper "-e-", as follows:

بزرگ

bozorg

big

كتاب بزرگ

ketaub-e-bozorg

the big book

جوان

javaun

young

مرد جوان

mard-e-javaun

young man

The second type of phrase is "the book is big", "the man is happy", "apples are red", "the people are British", etc. To form phrases like these, descriptors appear with a word like "is", "are", or "was". We shall look at how to "is", "are", and "was" etc in Chapter Two; for now, just remember that the word "*hast*" in the following examples means "is":

کتاب بزرگ هست

ketaub bozorg hast
the book is big

مرد جوان هست

mard javaun hast
the man is young

Here, note that the word for "is" appears right at the end of the whole phrase (unlike in English). The reason for this is explored in the next section.

Actions

Actions are words that refer, evidently, to actions. These actions can be simple physical actions like "run", "jump", "see", "think", etc or more abstract actions like "be", "become", "have", "seem", etc. The most important thing to remember about actions is that each action has two forms in Persian. For example, the action denoting "see" is "*bin \ did*". The first form is "*bin*", and the second form is "*did*". When learning any action in Persian, you should learn both forms right at the outset. Now this may sound like a lot to learn, given that for every one action in English, you must learn two different words in Persian, but in my view it is by far the most efficient way to learn actions in Persian. This is because actions in Persian are extremely regular; so long as you have learned the two forms for any given action, you will be able to form all the different expressions associated with that action, such as "will see", "saw", "have seen", "used to see", etc.

You cannot do this if (as suggested in other grammar books) you learn something called the "infinitive" form: *"didan"* – "to see", *"raftan"* – "to go", *"khordan"* – "to eat", etc. As will be discussed later, not only does this form not actually give you the first form of an action (and so does not enable you to say half the expressions you should be able to say), but the "infinitive" form is not even an action at all; it is in fact an object. Equally, standard translations of the "infinitive", such as "to see", "to go", "to eat", etc, are often problematic—in the way that those phrases are usually translated in Persian at least. Again, this is an example of traditional grammatical conventions being misapplied to languages that neither need them nor fit them. For now, just remember not to learn anything called an "infinitive"!

Talking about when an action happens

To denote when an action happens, either the first or second form of an action is used with certain helpers. These combinations are illustrated in the following examples, in which we will use the action *"bin \ did"* – "see" as our template:

می بین
mi bin
sees

دید
did
saw

می دید
mi did
used to see

These combinations can be made negative by adding the helper "*na…*", as follows:

نمی بین

نديد

*na*mi bin

*na*did

does not see

did not see

نمی ديد

*na*mi did

did not use to see

Talking about who performs an action

To denote who performs an action, simply use an object before the action (just as in English). Here, add the helper "*…ad*" to the first form of the action, as follows:

مرد می بيند

او ديد

*mard mi bin**ad***

u did

the man sees

he saw

If the performer of the action is more than one thing, add instead the helper "*…and*" to both forms of the action, as follows:

مردها می بينند

آنها ديدند

*mardhau mi bin**and***

*aunhau did**and***

the men see

they saw

Once you have learned what each combination of helper plus first or second form means, it is simple enough to substitute other actions for "*bin \ did*":

خور \ خورد
khor \ khord
eat

زن می خورد
*zan mi **khor**ad*
the woman eats

نویس \ نوشت
nevis \ nevesht
write

مردها نمی نویسند
*mardhau nami **nevis**and*
the men do not write

The order of words in a phrase

As mentioned above, the object denoting who is performing an action appears before that action (just as in English):

زنها آمدند
zanhau *aumadand*
the women came

In Persian, anything else appears between the two. This is why in the previous section, there was a different order from English in phrases like "the book is big" and "the man is young" etc:

زنها از ایران آمدند
*zanhau **az Iraun** aumadand*
the women came from Iran

"is seeing", "are seeing", "was seeing"

Note that *"mi bin"* – "sees" and *"mi did"* – "used to see" can also be used to denote "is seeing" and "was seeing" respectively. Likewise, *"nami bin"* and *"nami did"* can denote "is not seeing" and "was not seeing" respectively:

او می بیند

u mi binad

he is seeing

او نمی بیند

u nami binad

she is not seeing

مردها می دیدند

mardhau mi didand

the men were seeing

زنها نمی دیدند

zanhau nami didand

the women were not seeing

Note that this situation is different from English, in which an action such as "is", "are", or "was" etc is used with a descriptor such as "seeing", "eating", or "going" etc; unlike in Persian, there is in English absolutely no structural difference between phrases like "he is seeing", "he is seen", and "he is happy".

Asking questions

To ask a question, simply use the helper *"auyau"* before a whole phrase; do not reverse the order of the words as in English:

مرد می بیند

mard mi binad

the man sees

آیا مرد می بیند؟

Auyau mard mi binad?

Does the man see?

Special objects

With "*man*" – "I", "*mau*" – "we", or "*tou*" or "*shomau*" – "you", the helpers "*...ad*" and "*...and*" are not used. Instead, "*...am*", "*...im*", "*...i*", and "*...id*" are used respectively and in all instances:

من می بینم

man *mi binam*

I see

ما دیدیم

mau *didim*

we saw

تو می دیدی

tou *mi didi*

you used to see

شما نمی بینید

shomau *nami binid*

you do not see

In other grammar books, you will read about "first person", "second person", and "third person". Unless you want to be a linguist and describe lots of different languages in the same terms, you won't ever need to know what these phrases mean. Essentially, they are terms for describing phrases that are about the person speaking ("first person"), the person spoken to ("second person"), and the person spoken about ("third person"). A lot is made of these differences in many language books, but in my view, the changes that occur to actions depending on "person" can (in all the languages that I have studied) be best described as simply exceptions that occur with certain objects; in the case of Persian, these objects are "*man*", "*mau*", "*tou*", and "*shomau*". The fact that these objects and their equivalents are some of the most common objects in any given language does not necessitate three structural categories such as "first person", "second person", and "third person". All you need to remember is that when actions occur with a small number of special objects, they take different helpers.

Adding the helper "*be…*"

There is one more helper that is attached to actions in a similar manner to "*mi*", "*nami*", and "*na…*"; this is the helper "*be…*". This helper only appears with the first form of an action, as follows:

بین \ دید

bin \ did

see

مرد ببیند

mard bebinad

نویس \ نوشت

nevis \ nevesht

write

من بنویسم

man benevisam

In a similar manner, the helper "*na…*" can also be used with the first form of the action, as follows:

بین \ دید

bin \ did

see

مرد نبیند

mard nabinad

خور \ خورد

khor \ khord

eat

زن نخورد

zan nakhorad

Please note that I have not given a translation for either of these combinations because they only occur in certain special phrases. In my view, it is simpler not to translate these combinations; just remember that you need to use them in certain phrases only.

Again, this is not the approach you will find in most grammar books, which needlessly force a translation and label (such as "subjunctive", "conditional", or even "jussive") onto what are more efficiently learned as essentially meaningless phrases; in my view, it is easier to learn simply how these combinations are formed rather than trying to remember a confusing and flawed translation. Of course, what you do need to learn is in which special phrases these combinations appear; these phrases will all be detailed in Chapter Four.

Chapter Two: Elementary Rules

The rules in this chapter expand upon the more basic rules discussed in the last chapter. There are five sections; the first four sections each discuss additional rules about one category of word (objects, helpers, descriptors, and actions respectively), and the fifth section discusses additional rules about pronunciation.

Objects: Objects appearing as one thing

When it is obvious that an object denotes more than one thing, there is no need to add the helper "...*hau*". This usually occurs with numbers (see the next section) or when a helper makes it clear that more than one object is denoted:

كتابها

*ketaub**hau***

books

سه كتاب

se ketaub

three books

چند كتاب؟

cand ketaub?

how many books?

چندين كتاب

candin ketaub

several books

Objects with *"tau"*

When an object is used after the helper *"cand"*, the meaningless helper *"tau"* is inserted between *"cand"* and the object; this also occurs with numbers:

چند تا کتاب

*cand **tau** ketaub*

some books

چند تا کتاب؟

*cand **tau** ketaub?*

how many books?

دو تا کتاب

*dou **tau** ketaub*

two books

پنج تا کتاب

*panj **tau** ketaub*

five books

Helpers: The helper *"rau"*

As mentioned earlier, when studying another language, there are often words that are difficult or impossible to translate; in my view, it is misleading to try to translate these words. The helper *"rau"* is such a word. This helper appears after any object that is affected by an action. In a phrase like "the man eats the apple" for example, the object that is affected by the action is "apple" because it is the thing that is being eaten; likewise, in a phrase like "I saw him", the object that is affected by the action is "him" because "him" is the thing that was seen:

مرد سیب را می خورد

*mard sib **rau** mi khorad*

the man eats the apple

من او را دیدم

*man u **rau** didam*

I saw him

However, if "**an** apple" or "**a** woman" etc is specifically denoted, the helper "*rau*" is not used:

مرد یک سیب می خورد   من یک زن دیدم

mard yek sib mi khorad   *man yek zan didam*

the man eats an apple   I saw a woman

Note that when "*rau*" appears after the object "*man*", both words combine into "*marau*". Likewiese, when "*rau*" appears after the object "*tou*", both combine into "*torau*":

تو مرا می بینی   او کتاب مرا می خواند

*tou **marau** mi bini*   *u ketaub-e-**marau** mi khaunad*

you see me   he reads my book

من ترا می بینم   او کتاب ترا می خواند

*man **torau** mi binam*   *u ketaub-e-**torau** mi khaunad*

I see you   he reads your book

Alternatives to "-e-"

As described in Chapter One, the helper "-e-" appears between two objects to denote that the first object belongs to the second:

کتاب مرد   کتاب من

ketaub-e-mard   *ketaub-e-man*

the man's book   my book

When the second object is "*u*", "*aun*", "*aunhau*", "*man*", "*mau*", "*tou*", or "*shomau*", the following helpers can be used as alternatives:

كتاب او *ketaub-e-u* his book	كتابش *ketaubash* his book
كتاب او *ketaub-e-u* her book	كتابش *ketaubash* her book
كتاب آن *ketaub-e-aun* its book	كتابش *ketaubash* its book
كتاب آنها *ketaub-e-aunhau* their book	كتابشان *ketaubeshaun* their book
كتاب من *ketaub-e-man* my book	كتابم *ketaubam* my book
كتاب ما *ketaub-e-mau* our book	كتابمان *ketaubemaun* our book

کتاب تو

ketaub-e-tou
your book

کتابت

ketaubat
your book

کتاب شما

ketaub-e-shomau
your book

کتابتان

*ketaube**taun***
your book

The only difference between the two types of phrase is that the first type (with "-*e-*") is not used when the person who owns the object is also the person who is performing the action; in the following example, using a phrase with "-*e-*" would be impossible:

من سیبم را می خورم

man sibam rau mi khoram
I eat my apple

Logically, both alternatives are of course possible when talking about someone else:

مرد سیب او را می خورد

mard sib-e-u rau mi khorad
the man eats his apple ~someone else's apple

مرد سیبش را می خورد

mard sibash rau mi khorad
the man eats his apple ~his own apple

Finally, note helpers like the following:

پشت

posht-e-
behind

نزدیک

nazdik-e-
near

As you can see, these helpers all contain the helper "-*e*-"; therefore, alternatives with "...*ash*", "...*eshaun*", "...*am*", "...*emaun*", etc are all possible:

پشت او

posht-e-u
behind him

پشتش

*posht**ash***
behind him

نزدیک ما

nazdik-e-mau
near us

نزدیکمان

*nazdik**emaun***
near us

The helper "-*e*-" in complex phrases

When using the helper "-*e*-", it is sometimes difficult to keep track of multiple objects, descriptors, and helpers. Always remember that a phrase with "-*e*-" appears as one unit; this is a rule that intuitively makes sense:

کتاب بزرگ

ketaub-e-bozorg
the big book

کتاب بزرگ مرد

***ketaub-e-bozorg**-e-mard*
the man's big book

کتاب بزرگم
ketaub-e-bozorgam
my big book

کتاب بزرگ من
ketaub-e-bozorg-e-man
my big book

کتاب مرد بزرگ
ketaub-e-mard-e-bozorg
the big man's book

مرد بزرگ
mard-e-bozorg
the big man

او کتاب بزرگ مرا دید
*u **ketaub-e-bozorg-e-ma**rau did*
he saw my big book

او مرد بزرگ را دید
*u **mard-e-bozorg** rau did*
he saw the big man

کتاب برادر مرد
ketaub-e-baraudar-e-mard
the man's brother's book

برادر مرد
baraudar-e-mard
the man's brother

کتاب جدید بزرگ
ketaub-e-jadid-e-bozorg
the big new book

کتاب جدید جدید
ketaub -e-jadid
the new book

Note that the second object can occur with helpers that may appear to "break up" the phrase with "-e-". This is not the case; these combinations themselves should be considered one unit, as in the following examples:

کتاب آن مرد
*ketaub-e-**aun** mard*
that man's book

کتاب خیلی بزرگ
*ketaub-e-**cheili** bozorg*
the very big book

Numbers

Numbers are helpers; in Persian, they can appear by themselves (when counting for example) or before an object:

یک، دو، سه، چهار
yek, do, se, cahaur
one, two, three, four

دو کتاب
dou *ketaub*
two books

You should learn the following numbers in Persian:

یک
yek
one

دو
do
two

سه
se
three

چهار
cahaur
four

پنج
panj
five

شش
shesh
six

هفت
haft
seven

هشت
hasht
eight

نـه
noh
nine

ده
dah
ten

یازده
yauzdah
eleven

دوازده
davauzdah
twelve

سیزده
sizdah
thirteen

چهارده
cahaurdah
fourteen

پانزده
paunzdah
fifteen

شانزده
shaunzdah
sixteen

هفده
hefdah
seventeen

هجده
hejdah
eighteen

نوزده
nuzdah
nineteen

بیست
bist
twenty

سی
si
thirty

چهل
cehel
forty

پنجاه
panjauh
fifty

شصت
shasst
sixty

هفتاد
haftaud
seventy

هشتاد
hashtaud
eighty

نود
navad
ninety

صد
sád
one hundred

دویست
devist
two hundred

سیصد
sissad
three hundred

پانصد
paunssad
five hundred

هزار
hezaur
one thousand

All other numbers are expressed through simple combinations of the above words with the helper "*o*", as follows:

بیست و یک
bist o yek
twenty one

چهل و پنج
cehel o panj
forty five

دویست و شصت و دو   پانصد و هفت

devist o shasst o dou   *paunssad o haft*

two hundred and sixty two   five hundred and seven

چهار هزار و سیصد و سی و چهار

cahaur hezaur o sissad o si o cahaur

four thousand three hundred and thirty four

پنجاه هزار و دویست و هجده

panjauh hezaur o devist o hejdah

fifty thousand two hundred and eighteen

Note that unlike *"devist"*, *"sissad"*, and *"paunssad"*, the other numbers for the hundreds are all regularly formed:

شش صد   چهار صد و شانزده

shesh sád   *cahaur sád o shaunzdah*

six hundred   four hundred and sixteen

As you can see, numbers are extremely regular in Persian (as in fact they are in English); once you have learned the limited set of *unique* numbers, the other *constructed* numbers are expressed logically with *"o"*. This is not always the case in other languages; in Urdu, for instance, all numbers from one to 100 are unique. In Persian, there are 32 unique numbers to learn; in English, there are only 28.

"seventh", "eighth", "ninth"

To say "seventh" instead of "seven" or "fourteenth" instead of "fourteen", etc, simply add either the helper "...*om*" or the helper "...*omin*" to any number:

هفتم

haftom

seventh

هفتمین

haftomin

seventh

Both forms are used with objects. Numbers with "...*om*" always appear after an object and with the helper "-*e*-":

مرد هفتم

mard-e-haftom

the seventh man

کتاب بیست و پنجم

ketaub-e-bist o panjom

the twenty-fifth book

However, numbers with "...*omin*" only appear before objects:

هفتمین مرد

haftomin mard

the seventh man

بیست و پنجمین کتاب

bist o panjomin ketaub

the twenty-fifth book

To say "second", use the special forms "*dovom*" or "*dovomin*":

مرد دوّم

mard-e-dovom

the second man

دوّمین مرد

dovomin mard

the second man

بیست و دوّمین مرد   مرد بیست و دوّم
*bist o **dovomin** mard*   *mard-e-bist o **dovom***
the twenty-second man   the twenty-second man

Likewise, "third" is *"sevom"* or *"sevomin"*:

سوّمین مرد   مرد سوّم
sevomin** mard*   *mard-e-**sevom
the third man   the third man

بیست و سوّمین مرد   مرد بیست و سوّم
*bist o **sevomin** mard*   *mard-e-bist o **sevom***
the twenty-third man   the twenty-third man

For "first", *"aval"* and *"avalin"* are used:

اوّلین مرد   مرد اوّل
avalin** mard*   *mard-e-**aval
the first man   the first man

However, the regular form is used in constructed numbers like "twenty-first" or "thirty-first" etc:

بیست و یکمین مرد   مرد بیست و یکم
*bist o **yekomin** mard*   *mard-e-bist o **yekom***
the twenty-first man   the twenty-first man

Descriptors: Comparing things

Descriptors can be used to compare objects; you can say "younger" instead of "young", "bigger" instead of "big", "more beautiful" instead of "beautiful", etc. To do this in Persian, simply add the helper "...tar" to any descriptor:

جوانتر

*javaun**tar***

younger

زیباتر

*zibau**tar***

more beautiful

To say "biggest", "youngest", or "most beautiful" etc, add the helper "...tarin":

جوانترین

*javaun**tarin***

youngest

زیباترین

*zibau**tarin***

most beautiful

Descriptors with "...tar" are used just like any other descriptor; however, descriptors with "...tarin" only appear before objects:

کتاب بزرگتر

ketaub-e-bozorgtar

the bigger book

کتاب بزرگتر هست

ketaub bozorgtar hast

the book is bigger

بزرگترین کتاب

bozorgtarin *ketaub*

the biggest book

جوانترین زن

javauntarin *zan*

the youngest woman

Actions: Special actions

As mentioned earlier, all actions in Persian are extremely regular. Compared to many other languages, there are only a very small number of "special" actions in Persian—by which I mean actions that have exceptional rules associated with them. I do not want to use the term "irregular", which is used in many other grammar books; in my view, there are no irregular actions in Persian, just as there are no (or very few) irregular actions in many of the other languages in which this label is needlessly applied. In fact, there are only two special actions in Persian: *"daur \ dausht"* – "have" and *"baush \ bud"* – "be", but even the rules associated with these actions are quite straightforward. Use *"daur \ dausht"* and *"baush \ bud"* as you would any other action but remove any instance of the letters *MI* in their accompanying helpers:

من دارم

man ~~mi~~-dauram

I have

من ندارم

*man **nami**-dauram*

I do not have

من داشتم

man daushtam

I had

من نداشتم

man nadaushtam

I did not have

من داشتم

man ~~mi~~-daushtam

I used to have

من نداشتم

*man **nami**-daushtam*

I did not use to have

من باشم
*man **mi**-bausham*
~not used

من نباشم
*man **nami**-bausham*
~not used

من بودم
man budam
I was

من نبودم
man nabudam
I was not

من بودم
*man **mi**-budam*
I used to be

من نبودم
*man **nami**-budam*
I did not use to be

The above combinations that are labelled "not used" are replaced by the special forms *"hast"* and *"nist"* respectively:

مردها نیستند
*mardhau **nist**and*
the men are not

ما نیستیم
*mau **nist**im*
we are not

Note that the helper *"...ad"* is never used with *"hast"* and *"nist"*:

مرد هست
mard hast
the man is

او نیست
u nist
he is not

If you remember from Chapter One, the helpers *"be..."* and *"na..."* can also be used with the first form of an action. These helpers are only used in certain specific phrases (which will be described in Chapter Four). When *"be..."* is used with the first form *"baush"*, *"be..."* is removed:

او نباشد
*u **na**baushad*

او باشد
*u **be**baushad*

When *"be..."* is used with the first form *"daur"*, both combine into *"daushte baush"*; likewise, with *"na..."*, both combine into *"nadaushte baush"*:

او نداشته باشد
*u **nadaushte baush**ad*

او داشته باشد
*u **daushte baush**ad*

Omission of *"hast"*

In English, we can say "isn't" instead of "is not" or "I'm" instead of "I am", etc; likewise, the special form *"hast"* can also appear shortened in Persian. Simply remove the *"hast"* part of the action and add whatever remains to the previous word, as follows:

مردها جوان هستند
mardhau javaun hastand
the men are young

مردها جوانند
*mardhau javaun**and***
the men're young

من جوان هستم
man javaun hastam
I am young

من جوانم
*man javaun**am***
I'm young

ما جوان هستیم
mau javaun hastim
we are young

ما جوانیم
*mau javaun**im***
we're young

تو جوان هستی
tou javaun hasti
you are young

تو جوانی
*tou javaun**i***
you're young

شما جوان هستید
shomau javaun hastid
you are young

شما جوانید
*shomau javaun**id***
you're young

Note that *"hast"* itself shortens to *"ast"*:

مرد جوان هست
mard javaun hast
the man is young

مرد جوان است
*mard javaun **ast***
the man's young

After a word ending in a vowel, *"ast"* becomes *"...st"*:

آن زن زیباست
*aun zan zibau**st***
that woman is beautiful

کتاب نزدیک صندلیست
*ketaub nazdik-e-sándali**st***
the book is near the chair

Pronunciation: Pronouncing parts of words more strongly

In English, some parts of words are pronounced more strongly than others. In the English word "garden" for example, the first part of the word is pronounced more strongly: "GARden". In another word, like "computer", the middle part of the word is pronounced more strongly: "comPUter". Although the same thing happens in Persian, the situation is much simpler (as usual). In Persian, the last part of any word is pronounced more strongly:

كتاب

ketaub

"keTAUB"

جوان

javaun

"jaVAUN"

Helpers that are attached to other words are not considered part of the word; the last part of the original word is still pronounced more strongly:

كتابش

ketaubash

"keTAUBash"

من جوانم

man javaunam

"man jaVAUNam"

However, the helpers "...hau", "...tar", "...tarin", "...om", and "...omin" are considered part of the original word:

كتابها

ketaubhau

"ketaubHAU"

مردها

mardhau

"mardHAU"

جوانتر
javauntar
"javaunTAR"

جوانترین
javauntarin
"javauntaRIN"

پنجم
panjom
"panJOM"

پنجمین
panjomin
"panjoMIN"

Actions and their helpers are also pronounced as one word; however, they are pronounced more strongly on the first part of that word:

مرد می بیند
mard mi binad
"mard MIBinad"

من دیدم
man didam
"man DIDam"

تو هستی
tou hasti
"tou HASti"

ما نرفتیم
mau naraftim
"mau NARaftim"

Finally, note that the helper "*-e-*" is pronounced as part of the preceding word and not the following word, as follows:

کتاب بزرگ
ketaub-e-bozorg
"keTAUBe boZORG"

کتاب من
ketaub-e-man
"keTAUBe man"

Y insertion

When attaching helpers to other words, if two vowels come together, a *Y* is inserted between them:

من نمی گوید

man nami guyam
I do not say

آنها اینجایند

aunhau injauyand
they are here

او نیامد

u nayaumad
he did not come

او بیاید

u biauyad

Note that in the final example above, what should be "*bey...*" is written "*bi...*", which reflects the pronunciation more accurately. Note also that after a word ending in the letter *E*, any helper is usually written detached:

گربه ها

gorbe hau
cats

خسته تر

chaste tar
more tired

This means that in this instance, a *Y* is not inserted to separate vowel sounds; they usually combine into one, as follows:

گربه اش

"*gorbash*"
his cat

خسته ام

"*chastam*"
I am tired

Chapter Three: Words

This chapter contains a list of several hundred common words in Persian; this list is divided into four sub-lists: objects, helpers, descriptors, and actions. Objects and helpers are further divided into groups of related words. This list is essentially a foundation; you should continue to add to it as you encounter new words (see the Conclusion for some suggestions about continuing to improve your Persian after finishing this book). Note that some of the symbols used in these lists may need some explanation. The symbol ~ is used to clarify the meaning of a word, where a translation may otherwise be ambiguous:

خرما	*chormau*	date ~fruit
تاریخ	*taurich*	date ~time

The symbol / shows there are multiple translations of the same word; it essentially means "or":

مغازه / دکان	*maghauze / dokaun*	shop
توی / در	*tu-e- / dar*	in

The first form of an action is listed before the second form:

خوان \ خواند	*khaun \ khaund*	study
گیر \ گرفت	*gir \ gereft*	take

The symbol | always appears before a word in both the Persian and English translations; it denotes that both words correspond to each other:

فارسی	*Faursi ǀbe*	Persian ǀin
ممنون	*mamnun ǀaz*	grateful ǀfor

به فارسی

be Faursi

in Persian

ممنون از این کتاب

mamnun **az** in ketaub

grateful for this book

The names for people remain untranslated:

فرشته	*Fereshte*
احمد	*Ahhmad*

The months of the Persian calendar are also untranslated, though they are listed in chronological order:

فروردین	*Farvardin*
اردیبهشت	*Ordibehesht*

As described in Chapter One, an object appears with the helper
"...*hau*" when denoting more than one thing:

کتابها

*ketaub**hau***

books

مردها

*mard**hau***

men

However, some objects may change to a different form when
denoting more than one thing; in this case, the form these objects
change into has been listed as follows:

| شخص < اشخاص | *shachss > ashchauss* | person |
| میوه < میوه جات | *mive > mive jaut* | fruit |

In a similar manner, objects denoting human beings can also
appear in a different form; this usually occurs by adding the helper
"...*aun*" instead of "...*hau*". However, these special forms have not
been listed because this is a relatively systematic change:

مردها

mardhau

men

مردان

*mard**aun***

men

زنها

zanhau

women

زنان

*zan**aun***

women

In either case, always remember that these forms are optional; the normal method of adding "...*hau*" is always acceptable:

شخصها

shachsshau

people

اشخاص

ashchauss

people

مردها

mardhau

men

مردان

mardaun

men

Another reason why I have not listed all of these special forms is that in general, you should completely avoid using them. Few of these forms are used in modern Persian anyway, and using anything other than "...*hau*" to talk about more than one thing in everyday conversation may sound very formal (see Chapter Five for a discussion of "formal" and "informal" Persian).

Objects: Basic objects

لهجه	*lahje*	accent
تصادف	*tassaudof*	accident
نشانی	*neshauni*	address
ابلاغیه	*eblaughie*	advice
بعد از ظهر	*bajhd az dzohr*	afternoon
سن	*sen*	age ~years old
فرودگاه	*forudgauh*	airport
سفیر	*safir*	ambassador
آمبولانس	*aumbulauns*	ambulance
حیوان	*héivaun*	animal
جواب	*javaub*	answer
آپارتمان	*aupaurtamaun*	apartment
سیب	*sib*	apple
عربی	*Árabi*	Arabic
بازو	*bauzu*	arm
پاییز	*pauyiz*	autumn
کیف	*kif*	bag
بانک	*baunk*	bank
تختخواب	*tachtekhaub*	bed
اتاق خواب	*otauq-e-khaub*	bedroom
پرنده	*parande*	bird
قایق	*qauyeq*	boat
بدن	*badan*	body
کتاب	*ketaub*	book
کتاب فروشی	*ketaub forushi*	bookshop
پوتین	*putin*	boot
نان	*naun*	bread
زنگ تفریح	*zang-e-tafrihh*	break ~rest
صبحانه	*sóbhhaune*	breakfast

برادر	baraudar	brother
ساختمان	sauchtemaun	building
اتوبوس	otubus	bus
کره	kare	butter
کافه	kaufe	cafe
ماشین	maushin	car
فرش	farsh	carpet
هویج	havij	carrot
گربه	gorbe	cat
صندلی	sándali	chair
پنیر	panir	cheese
چک بانکی	cek-e-baunki	cheque
مرغ	morgh	chicken
بچه	bace	child
شکلات	shokolaut	chocolate
کلیسا	kelisau	church
سیگار	sigaur	cigarette
سینما	sinamau	cinema
شهر	shahr	city
کلاس	kelaus	class
لباس	lebaus	clothes
قهوه	qahve	coffee
قهوه خانه	qahve chaune	coffeeshop
کامپیوتر	kaumpiuter	computer
کشور	keshvar	country ~nation
خامه	chaume	cream
کارت اعتباری	kaurt-e-ejhtebauri	credit card
فنجان	fenjaun	cup
پرده	parde	curtain
بابا	baubau	dad
خرما	chormau	date ~fruit

تاریخ	*taurich*	date ~time
دختر	*dochtar*	daughter
روز	*ruz*	day
تصمیم	*tassmim*	decision
دندانپزشک	*dandaunpezeshk*	dentist
بیابان	*biaubaun*	desert
دسر	*deser*	dessert
شام	*shaum*	dinner
ظرف	*dzarf*	dish
پزشک	*pezeshk*	doctor
سگ	*sag*	dog
در	*dar*	door
کشو	*kesho*	drawer
راننده	*raunande*	driver
گوش	*gush*	ear
شرق	*sharq*	east
تخم مرغ	*tochm-e-morgh*	egg
مهندس	*mohandes*	engineer
انگلیسی	*Engelisi*	English
شب	*shab*	evening
امتحان	*emtehhaun*	examination
مثال	*meszaul*	example
چشم	*ceshm*	eye
چهره	*cehre*	face
کارخانه	*kaurchaune*	factory
خانواده	*chaunevaude*	family
مزرعه	*mazrajhe*	farm
پدر	*pedar*	father
احساس	*ehhsaus*	feeling
چمنزار	*camanzaur*	field
فیلم	*film*	film

انگشت	angosht	finger
آتش	autash	fire
ماهی	mauhi	fish
طبقه	dtabaqe	floor ~storey
غذا	ghaxau	food
پا	pau	foot
چنگال	cangaul	fork
فرانسوی	Faraunsavi	French
دوست	dust	friend
میوه > میوه جات	mive > mive jaut	fruit
بازی	bauzi	game
باغ	baugh	garden
سیر	sir	garlic
لیوان	livaun	glass ~tumbler
نوه	nave	grandchild
نوه ی دختری	nave-e-dochtari	granddaughter
پدر بزرگ	pedar-e-bozorg	grandfather
مادر بزرگ	maudar-e-bozorg	grandmother
نوه ی پسری	nave-e-pesari	grandson
چمن	caman	grass
گروه	goruh	group
مهمان	mehmaun	guest
دست	dast	hand
کیف دستی	kif-e-dasti	handbag
کلاه	kolauh	hat
سر	sar	head
سردرد	sardard	headache
تپه	tape	hill
سفر تفریحی	safar-e-tafrihhi	holiday ~trip
خانه / منزل	chaune / manzel	home
تکلیف	taklif	homework

اسب	asb	horse
بیمارستان	bimaurestaun	hospital
هتل	hotel	hotel
خانه / منزل	chaune / manzel	house
شوهر	shouhar	husband
بستنی	bastani	ice cream
اطلاعات	ettelaujhaut	information
جزیره	jazire	island
ژاکت	zhaukat	jacket
شغل	shoghl	job
مسافرت	mosauferat	journey
کلید	kelid	key
آشپزخانه	aushpazchaune	kitchen
چاقو	cauqu	knife
خانم	chaunom	lady
زبان	zabaun	language
رهبر	rahbar	leader
کتابخانه	ketaubchaune	library
چراغ	ceraugh	light ~lamp
اسباب	asbaub	luggage
ناهار	nauhaur	lunch
خانم	chaunom	madam
مرد	mard	man
مدیر	modir	manager
نقشه	naqshe	map
بازار	bauzaur	market
مفهوم	mafhum	meaning
گوشت	gusht	meat
دارو	dauru	medicine ~drugs
جلسه	jalase	meeting
پیام	payaum	message

شیر	shir	milk
دقیقه	daqiqe	minute
آینه	auyene	mirror
پول	pul	money
ماه	mauh	month
صبح	sóbhh	morning
مسجد	masjed	mosque
مادر	maudar	mother
موتورسیکلت	moutoursiklet	motorbike
کوه	kuh	mountain
دهان	dahaun	mouth
مامان	maumaun	mum
موزه	muze	museum
موسیقی	musiqi	music
اسم	esm	name
گردن	gardan	neck
همسایه	hamsauye	neighbour
خبر	chabar	news
روزنامه	ruznaume	newspaper
شب	shab	night
شمال	shomaul	north
بینی	bini	nose
اداره	edaure	office
پیاز	piauz	onion
نظر	nadzar |be	opinion |in
کاغذ	kaughax	paper
والدین	vauledein	parents
پارک	paurk	park
گذرنامه	goxarnaume	passport
خودکار	khodkaur	pen
مداد	medaud	pencil

مردم	mardom	people
فارسی	Faursi |be	Persian |in
شخص < اشخاص	shachss > ashchauss	person
عکس	áks	photograph
تصویر	tassvir	picture
جا	jau	place
بشقاب	boshqaub	plate
جیب	jib	pocket
پلیس	polis	police
پاسبان	pausebaun	policeman
سیاستمدار	siausatmadaur	politician
پستخانه	postchaune	post office
سیب زمینی	sib zamini	potato
قیمت	qeimat	price
کیف پول	kif-e-pul	purse
سوال	souaul	question
رادیو	raudio	radio
دین	din	religion
رستوران	rasturaun	restaurant
پلو	polo	rice
رودخانه	rudchaune	river
جاده	jaude	road
بام	baum	roof
اتاق	otauq	room
سالاد	saulaud	salad
نمک	namak	salt
ساندویچ	saundvic	sandwich
مدرسه	madrase	school
دریا	dariau	sea
منشی	monshi	secretary
ملافه	malaufe	sheet

کشتی	keshti	ship
پیراهن	pirauhan	shirt
کفش	kafsh	shoe
مغازه / دکان	maghauze / dokaun	shop
دکاندار	dokaundaur	shopkeeper
شانه	shaune	shoulder
دوش	dush	shower
تابلو	taublo	sign
آقا	auqau	sir
خواهر	khauhar	sister
پوست	pust	skin
دامن	dauman	skirt
آسمان	ausemaun	sky
مار	maur	snake
پسر	pesar	son
سوپ	sup	soup
جنوب	jonub	south
عنکبوت	ánkabut	spider
قاشق	qaushoq	spoon
ورزش	varzesh	sport
بهار	bahaur	spring ~season
میدان	meidaun	square ~a place
ستاره	setaure	star
داستان	daustaun	story
خیابان	chiaubaun	street
چمدان	camedaun	suitcase
تابستان	taubestaun	summer
خورشید	khorshid	sun
فروشگاه	forushgauh	supermarket
میز	miz	table
تاکسی	tauksi	taxi

چای	caui	tea
معلم	mojhalem	teacher
تلفن	telefon	telephone
تلویزیون	televiziun	television
سارق	saureq	thief
چیز	ciz	thing
بلیط	belitt	ticket
وقت	vaqt	time
قوطی	qutti	tin ~container
توالت	tovaulet	toilet
گوجه فرنگی	gouje farangi	tomato
زبان	zabaun	tongue
دندان	dandaun	tooth
مسواک	mesvauk	toothbrush
خمیر دندان	chamir-e-dandaun	toothpaste
توریست	turist	tourist
برج	borj	tower
مرکز شهر	markaz-e-shahr	town centre
ترافیک	teraufik	traffic
درخت	deracht	tree
شلوار	shalvaur	trousers
آموزگار	aumuzgaur	tutor
دانشگاه	dauneshgauh	university
دره	dare	valley
واگن	vaugon	van
نما	namau	view ~scene
دهکده	dehkade	village
مهمان	mehmaun	visitor
پیشخدمت	pishchedmat	waiter
دیوار	divaur	wall
کیف پول	kif-e-pul	wallet

کمد	komod	wardrobe
آب	aub	water
طرف	dtaraf	way ~direction
هوا	havau	weather
هفته	hafte	week
آخر هفته	auchar-e-hafte	weekend
غرب	gharb	west
خانم	chaunom	wife
باد	baud	wind
پنجره	panjere	window
شراب	sharaub	wine
زمستان	zemestaun	winter
گرگ	gorg	wolf
زن	zan	woman
چوب	cub	wood ~material
کلمه	kalame	word
کار	kaur	work
کرم	kerm	worm
مچ دست	moc-e-dast	wrist
نویسنده	nevisande	writer
سال	saul	year
ماست	maust	yoghurt
باغ وحش	baugh-e-vahhsh	zoo

"he", "she", "it"

او	u	he
او	u	she
آن	aun	it
آنها	aunhau	they
من	man	I
ما	mau	we
تو	tou	you ~one person
شما	shomau	you ~more than one

"this", "these", "that"

این	in	this
اینها	inhau	these
آن	aun	that
آنها	aunhau	those

Objects used in questions

چی	ci	what?
کی	ki	who?
کی	kei	when?
کجا	kojau	where?
چطور	cettour	how?
چرا	cerau	why?
چند	cand	how many?
چقدر	ceqadr	how much?
مال کی	maul-e-ki	whose?

"anybody", "anything", "somebody"

هر کسی	*har kasi*	anybody
هر چیزی	*har cizi*	anything
کسی	*kasi*	somebody
چیزی	*cizi*	something
هیچکس	*hickas*	nobody
هیچ	*hic*	nothing
همه کس	*hame kas*	everybody
همه اش	*hamash*	everything

Objects denoting when something happens

امروز	*emruz*	today
فردا	*fardau*	tomorrow
دیروز	*diruz*	yesterday
امشب	*emshab*	this evening

دوباره	*doubaure*	again
هنوز	*hanuz*	already
همیشه	*hamishe*	always
زود	*zud*	early
هیچوقت	*hicvaqt*	never
الان	*alaun*	now
زیاد	*ziaud*	often
گهگاهی	*gahgauhi*	sometimes
به زودی	*be zudi*	soon
ناگهان	*naugahaun*	suddenly
معمولاً	*majhmulann*	usually

Objects denoting where something happens

اینجا	injau	here
آنجا	aunjau	there
داخل	dauchel	inside
بیرون	birun	outside
دست چپ	dast-e-cap	on the left
دست راست	dast-e-raust	on the right

Objects denoting how something happens

تنهایی	tanhauyi	alone
حتماً	hátmann	certainly
دقیقاً	daqiqann	exactly
خوشبختانه	khoshbachtaune	fortunately
شاید	shauyad	maybe
به سرعت	be sorjhat	quickly
به آرامی	be auraumi	quietly
آهسته	auheste	slowly
با هم	bau ham	together
خوب	khob	well

Unique numbers

صفر	séfr	zero
یک	yek	one
دو	dou	two
سه	se	three
چهار	cahaur	four
پنج	panj	five

شش	*shesh*	six
هفت	*haft*	seven
هشت	*hasht*	eight
نه	*noh*	nine
ده	*dah*	ten
یازده	*yauzdah*	eleven
دوازده	*davauzdah*	twelve
سیزده	*sizdah*	thirteen
چهارده	*cahaurdah*	fourteen
پانزده	*paunzdah*	fifteen
شانزده	*shaunzdah*	sixteen
هفده	*hefdah*	seventeen
هجده	*hejdah*	eighteen
نوزده	*nuzdah*	nineteen
بیست	*bist*	twenty
سی	*si*	thirty
چهل	*cehel*	forty
پنجاه	*panjauh*	fifty
شصت	*shasst*	sixty
هفتاد	*haftaud*	seventy
هشتاد	*hashtaud*	eighty
نود	*navad*	ninety
صد	*sád*	one hundred
دویست	*devist*	two hundred
سیصد	*sissad*	three hundred
پانصد	*paunssad*	five hundred
هزار	*hezaur*	one thousand
ملیون	*meliun*	one million

Countries, continents, and cities

افغانستان	*Afghaunestaun*	Afghanistan
بحرین	*Bahhrein*	Bahrain
برزیل	*Berzil*	Brazil
بریتانیا	*Britauniau*	Britain
کانادا	*Kaunaudau*	Canada
چین	*Cin*	China
مصر	*Messr*	Egypt
انگلستان	*Englestaun*	England
فرانسه	*Faraunse*	France
آلمان	*Aulmaun*	Germany
هند	*Hend*	India
ایران	*Iraun*	Iran
عراق	*Érauq*	Iraq
ایتالیا	*Itauliau*	Italy
ژاپن	*Zhaupon*	Japan
کویت	*Koveit*	Kuwait
عمان	*Ómaun*	Oman
پاکستان	*Paukestaun*	Pakistan
لهستان	*Lahestaun*	Poland
روسیه	*Rusie*	Russia
عربستان سعودی	*Árabestaun-e-Sajhudi*	Saudi Arabia
اسپانیا	*Espauniau*	Spain
سوریه	*Surie*	Syria
ترکیه	*Torkie*	Turkey
افریقا	*Efriqau*	Africa
آمریکا	*Aumrikau*	America
آسیا	*Ausiau*	Asia
اروپا	*Orupau*	Europe

تهران	*Tehraun*	Tehran
اصفهان	*Essfahaun*	Isfahan
شیراز	*Shirauz*	Shiraz

لندن	*Landan*	London
نیویورک	*Niuyourk*	New York
واشنگتن	*Vaushengton*	Washington

اهل کجا	*ahl-e-kojau*	what nationality?

Female names

دریا	*Dariau*
فرشته	*Fereshte*
مهتاب	*Mahtaub*
مونیره	*Munire*
پروانه	*Parvaune*
پروین	*Parvin*
سایه	*Sauye*
ستاره	*Setaure*
شبنم	*Shabnam*
شادی	*Shaudi*
سنبل	*Sonbol*
زری	*Zari*
زیبا	*Zibau*

Male names

احمد	*Ahhmad*
امین	*Amin*
خسرو	*Chosro*
فرهاد	*Farhaud*
حمید	*Hámid*
کریم	*Karim*
مانی	*Mauni*
محمد	*Mohhamad*
رضا	*Rezzau*
سعدی	*Sajhdi*
سیروس	*Sirus*
عباس	*Ábaus*
علی	*Áli*

Surnames

بهار	*Bahaur*
خان	*Chaun*
دیداری	*Didauri*
هادیان	*Haudiaun*
هدایت	*Hedauyat*
همایون	*Homauyun*
منوچهری	*Manucehri*
مشیری	*Moshiri*
موحدیان	*Movahhediaun*
نوشزاد	*Noushzaud*
پیامی	*Payaumi*
عباسی	*Ábausi*

Days and months

دوشنبه	*Doushanbe*	Monday
سه شنبه	*Se Shanbe*	Tuesday
چهارشنبه	*Cahaurshanbe*	Wednesday
پنجشنبه	*Panjshanbe*	Thursday
جمعه	*Jomjhe*	Friday
شنبه	*Shanbe*	Saturday
یکشنبه	*Yekshanbe*	Sunday
ژانویه	*Zhaunvie*	January
فوریه	*Fevrie*	February
مارچ	*Maurc*	March
آوریل	*Auvril*	April
مه	*Me*	May
ژوئن	*Zhuan*	June
ژوئیه	*Zhuie*	July
اوت	*Ut*	August
سپتامبر	*Septaumbr*	September
اکتبر	*Oktobr*	October
نوامبر	*Novaumbr*	November
دسامبر	*Desaumbr*	December
فروردین	*Farvardin*	
اردیبهشت	*Ordibehesht*	
خرداد	*Chordaud*	
تیر	*Tir*	
مرداد	*Mordaud*	
شهریور	*Shahrivar*	
مهر	*Mehr*	

آبان	Aubaun	
آذر	Auxar	
دی	Dei	
بهمن	Bahman	
اسفند	Esfand	

Amounts

یک کمی	yek kami	a little
همش	hamash	all of it
همه	hame	all
بیشتر	bishtar	more
یکی	yeki	one ~one thing

"the man's", "ours", "theirs"

مال مرد	maul-e-mard	the man's ~etc
مال ما	maul-e-mau	ours ~etc

"myself", "yourself", "each other"

خود من	khod-e-man	myself ~etc
همدیگر / یکدیگر	hamdigar / yekdigar	each other

Helpers: Helpers used before objects

کدام	kodaum	which?
این	in	this
این	in	these
آن	aun	that
آن	aun	those
هر دو	har dou	both
بالای	baulau-e-	above
در میان	dar miaun-e-	among
سر	sar-e-	at
پشت	posht-e-	behind
بین / میان	bein-e- / miaun-e-	between
از	az	from
توی / در	tu-e- / dar	in
جلوی	jelou-e-	in front of
داخل / درون	dauchel-e- / darun-e-	inside
نزدیک	nazdik-e-	near
کنار	kenaur-e-	next to
روی	ru-e-	on
در برابر	dar baraubar-e-	opposite
به	be	to
پیش / تا	pish-e- / tau	towards
زیر	zir-e-	under
چند	cand	how many?
چند	cand	how much?
چند	cand	a few
خیلی	cheili	a lot of

همه ی	hame-e-	all
تمام	tamaum-e-	all ~the whole of
تقریباً	taqribann	about ~amount
هر	har	each
خیلی از	cheili az	many of
بیشتر	bishtar	more
بیشتر	bishtar-e-	most of
یکی از	yeki az	one of
فقط	faqatt	only
چندین	candin	several
بعضی	bajhzzi	some ~several
بعضی از	bajhzzi az	some of
بعد از / پس از	bajhd az / pas az	after
پیش از / قبل از	pish az / qabl az	before
تا	tau	by ~a time
طی	dtei-e-	during
از	az	since
راجع به	raujejh be	about ~a topic
به سبب	be sabab-e-	because of
توسط	tavasot-e-	by ~done by
(به) جز	(be) joz	except
برای	barau-e-	for
به جای	be jau-e-	instead of
مثل	meszl-e-	like
با	bau	with
بدون / بی	bedun-e- / bi	without

آقای	Auqau-e-	Mr
خانم	Chaunom-e-	Mrs
دوشیزه ی	Dushize-e-	Miss

Helpers used after objects

کی	...-e-ki	whose ...?
ـم	...am	my ...
ـمان	...emaun	our ...
ـش	...ash	his ...
ـش	...ash	her ...
ـش	...ash	its ...
ـشان	...eshaun	their ...
ـت	...at	your ...
ـتان	...etaun	your ...
خود من	...-e-khod-e-man	my own ... ~etc

| زیادی | -e-ziaudi | many ... |
| دیگری | -e-digari | another ... |

| هم | ham | ... too |
| پیش | pish | ... ago |

Helpers that surround objects

| چه ـی | ce ...i | what ...? |
| چه جور ـی | ce jur ...i | what kind of ...? |

هم --- هم ---	*ham ... ham ...*	both ... and...
یا --- یا ---	*yau ... yau ...*	either... or ...
نه --- نه ---	*nah ... nah ...*	neither ... nor ...

Helpers used before descriptors

چقدر	*ceqadr*	how?
یک کمی	*yek kami*	a little
زیاد	*ziaud*	too
خیلی	*cheili*	very

Helpers used before whole phrases

| که | *ke* | that |

بعد از اینکه	*bajhd az inke*	after
قبل از اینکه	*qabl az inke*	before
از وقتی که	*az vaqti ke*	since
تا	*tau*	until
وقتی که / موقعی که	*vaqti ke / mouqejhi ke*	when

چون / چونکه	*cun / cunke*	because
اگرچه	*agarce*	although
مگر اینکه	*magar inke*	unless
در صورتی که	*dar súrati ke*	in case

| اگر | *agar* | if |
| پس | *pas* | then ~so |

Helpers used as in English

سلام	salaum	hello
خدا حافظ	Chodau háufedz	goodbye
صبح به خیر	sóbhh be cheir	good morning
ظهر به خیر	dzohr be cheir	good afternoon
عصر به خیر	ássr be cheir	good evening
شب به خیر	shab be cheir	good night
بله	bale	yes
نه	nah	no
آره	aure	yeah
البته	albate	of course
لطفاً	lottfann	please
مرسی	mersi	thank you
و	va	and
یا	yau	or
ولی	vali	but

Descriptors: Basic descriptors

ترسیده	tarside	afraid
تنها	tanhau	alone
خوب	chub	alright
عصبانی	ássabauni	angry
مناسب	monauseb	appropriate
خوابیده	khaubide	asleep
واقف	vauqef |be	aware |of
بد	bad	bad
زیبا	zibau	beautiful
بزرگ	bozorg	big
مشغول	mashghul	busy
ارزان	arzaun	cheap
تمیز	tamiz	clean
مشخص	moshachas	clear
زرنگ	zerang	clever
سرد	sard	cold
تمام	tamaum	complete
خطرناک	chattarnauk	dangerous
تاریک	taurik	dark
مشکل	moshkel	difficult
کثیف	kaszif	dirty
خشک	chosk	dry
زود	zud	early
آسان	ausaun	easy
خالی	chauli	empty
معروف	majhruf |be	famous |for
تند	tond	fast
چاق	cauq	fat
آزاد	auzaud	free

دوستانه	dustaune	friendly
خنده دار	chande daur	funny
خوب	chub	good
خوش قیافه	khosh qiaufe	good looking
ممنون	mamnun |az	grateful |for
عالى	áuli	great
خوش	khosh	happy
سخت	sacht	hard ~difficult
بیمار / مریض	bimaur / marizz	ill
مهم	mohem	important
غیر ممکن	gheir-e-momken	impossible
جالب	jauleb	interesting
بین المللى	bein olmelali	international
حسود	hásud	jealous
مهربان	mehrabaun	kind
درشت	dorosht	large
تنبل	tanbal	lazy
روشن	roushan	light
تنها	tanhau	lonely
دراز	derauz	long
دیوانه	divaune	mad
مدرن	modern	modern
واجب	vaujeb	necessary
عصبى	ássabi	nervous
جدید / نو	jadid / no	new
دلپذیر	delpaxir	nice
واضح	vauzzehh |bar	obvious |to
قدیمى	qadimi	old
باز	bauz	open
دردناک	dardnauk	painful
آرام	auraum	peaceful ~quiet

با ادب	bau adab	polite
سیاسی	siausi	political
بیچاره	bicaure	poor
ممکن	momken	possible
ساکت	sauket	quiet
حاضر	háuzzer	ready
دینی	dini	religious
پولدار	puldaur	rich ~wealthy
راست	raust	right ~correct
ناراحت	naurauhhat	sad
جدی	jedi	serious
کوچک	kucak	small
عجیب	ájib	strange
قوی	qavi	strong
احمق	ahhmaq	stupid
خسته	chaste	tired
سنتی	sonati	traditional
زشت	zesht	ugly
مفید	mofid	useful
ضعیف	zájhif	weak
خیس	chis	wet
پهن	pahn	wide
نگران	negaraun	worried
جوان	javaun	young

Colours

قرمز	qermez	red
آبی	aubi	blue
زرد	zard	yellow

سبز	*sabz*	green
سیاه	*siauh*	black
سفید	*sefid*	white
صورتی	*súrati*	pink
ارغوانی	*arghavauni*	purple
نارنجی	*naurenji*	orange
قهوه ای	*qahve i*	brown
خاکستری	*chaukestari*	grey

Nationalities

آمریکایی	*Aumrikauyi*	American
عربی	*Áarabi*	Arabic
بریتانیایی	*Britauniauyi*	British
اروپایی	*Orupauyi*	European
ایرانی	*Irauni*	Iranian

Other descriptors

| دیگر | *digar* | other |

| چندساله | *candsaule* | how old? |
| ده ساله | *dah saule* | ten years old |

Actions: Basic actions

ستا \ ستود	setau \ sotud	admire
رس \ رسید	res \ resid |be	arrive |in / at
پرس \ پرسید	pors \ porsid |az	ask |~someone
باش \ بود	baush \ bud	be
ترس \ ترسید	tars \ tarsid |az	be afraid |of
توان \ توانست	tavaun \ tavaunest	be able
شو \ شد	shav \ shod	become
سکن \ شکست	shekan \ shekast	break
آور \ آورد	auvar \ auvard	bring
ساز \ ساخت	sauz \ saucht	build
سوز \ سوخت	suz \ sucht	burn ~be on fire
سوزان \ سوزاند	suzaun \ suzaund	burn ~something
بر \ برد	bar \ bord	carry
بند \ بست	band \ bast	close
آ \ آمد	au \ aumad	come
پیوند \ پیوست	peivand \ peivast	connect
پز \ پخت	paz \ pocht	cook
بر \ برید	bor \ borid	cut
رقصان \ رقصاند	raqssaun \ raqssaund	dance
میر \ مرد	mir \ mord	die
نوش \ نوشید	nush \ nushid	drink
ران \ راند	raun \ raund	drive
ریز \ ریخت	riz \ richt	drop
خور \ خورد	khor \ khord	eat
زی \ زیست	zi \ zist	exist
فهمان \ فهماند	fahmaun \ fahmaund	explain
افت \ افتاد	oft \ oftaud	fall
پر \ پرید	par \ parid	fly
گرا \ گروید	gerau \ gerouid	follow

آمرز \ آمرزید	*aumorz \ aumorzid*	forgive
گیر \ گرفت	*gir \ gereft*	get ~something
ده \ داد	*dah \ daud |be*	give |~someone
رو \ رفت	*rav \ raft*	go
دار \ داشت	*daur \ dausht*	have
شنو \ شنید	*shenav \ shenid*	hear
زن \ زد	*zan \ zad*	hit
جه \ جهید	*jah \ jahid*	jump
کش \ کشت	*kosh \ kosht*	kill
بوس \ بوسید	*bus \ busid*	kiss
شناس \ شناخت	*shenaus \ shenaucht*	know ~a person
دان \ دانست	*daun \ daunest*	know ~a fact
خند \ خندید	*chand \ chandid |be*	laugh |at
کش \ کشید	*kesh \ keshid*	pull
گذار \ گزاشت	*goxaur \ goxausht*	put
خوان \ خواند	*khaun \ khaund*	read
گو \ گفت	*gu \ goft*	say
بین \ دید	*bin \ did*	see
فروش \ فروخت	*forush \ forucht*	sell
فرست \ فرستاد	*ferest \ ferestaud*	send
نشین \ نشست	*neshin \ neshast*	sit
مان \ ماند	*maun \ maund*	stay
خوان \ خواند	*khaun \ khaund*	study
گیر \ گرفت	*gir \ gereft*	take
گو \ گفت	*gu \ goft |be*	tell |~someone
فهم \ فهمید	*fahm \ fahmid*	understand
خواه \ خواست	*khauh \ khaust*	want
شو \ شست	*shu \ shost*	wash
پوش \ پوشید	*push \ pushid*	wear
نویس \ نوشت	*nevis \ nevesht*	write

Although the words in this chapter are only a very small fraction of the total number of words you will need to communicate effectively in Persian, you should have enough words to get your basic meaning across in many situations or understand the gist of some of the things you will hear or read; again, you should continue to add to this list as you practise. Remember that when you encounter a helper, you only need to make a note of what it means and where it goes; is the helper appearing before a descriptor for example, or is the helper being used after (and to give meaning to) an entire phrase? This is important because the English translation you assign to any particular helper might not correlate with its actual use in Persian. Compare, for example, the Persian helpers "*bajhd az inke*" and "*bajhd az*"; although both helpers can be translated by the English helper "after", "*bajhd az*" appears before an object in Persian and "*bajhd az inke*" appears before a whole phrase:

بعد از کلاس

bajhd az kelaus

after the class

بعد از اینکه او رفت

bajhd az inke u raft

after he went

Another important feature to note is the use of associated words (which are often helpers). In English, for example, we say "grateful **for**" something; in Persian, we use the helper "*az*" – "from": "*mamnun **az** cizi*". When you note down a new word, make sure to check if there are any differences in associated words like this. I have noted some of these in this chapter, but do continue to add other associated words as you encounter them.

Chapter Four: Elevations

An elevation is a mental tool for learning languages. It is designed to categorise a phrase that has an *actual* meaning that is different from its *literal* translation, the literal translation being analysed in terms of rules that are purposefully simpler than the rules that would otherwise be needed to analyse that phrase. Now, this sounds very complicated! But the concept really isn't that difficult once you get used to it. Let's start by considering an example:

man az ketaub khosham mi auyad

According to the rules described so far, the literal translation of this phrase is something like "I from the book my *'khosh'* comes". Clearly, this doesn't make much sense, and not just because we do not know what the word "*khosh*" means. Yet, however strange such a translation might appear, it is crucial to note that the rules we have learned so far do allow us to give the phrase this literal translation:

man az ketaub khosham mi auyad > I from the book my "*khosh*" comes

This phrase does in fact have an actual meaning in Persian; this meaning is "I like the book". The literal translation is *elevated* to denote "I like the book":

like the book

man az ketaub khosham mi auyad > I ~~from the book my "khosh" comes~~

We could of course create an explicit rule to describe this, such as "when the verb 'like' is denoted by *'aumadan'*, an experiencer subject is used, which is expressed by an isolated noun or pronoun occuring before the semantic object and a possessive pronoun suffix attached to the noun *'khosh'* (which acts as the grammatical subject of the verb); the grammatical object takes the preposition *'az'* and thus syntactically functions as an adjunct". Evidently, this is not the easiest way to learn how to say "I like the book" in Persian! (I have even seen resources written for English-speaking learners of foreign languages that seem to focus on teaching those learners about English grammar!) Instead of studying for a degree in Linguistics before we can learn how to say "I like the book", we can just remember this single example:

من از کتاب خوشم می آید

man az ketaub khosham mi auyad
I like the book

The key is the literal translation we were able to give the phrase earlier; you simply use the rules you have learned so far in this book to modify the literal translation in order to express a desired actual meaning. The fact that you may not know what *"khosh"* means has absolutely no bearing; you just need to recognise (from how it is used in the phrase) that it is an object.

The crucial advantage of doing this is that the rules we are using are all relatively simple, especially in comparison to the ones we would otherwise have to learn. Learning a whole new "language" of grammatical terminology is not why you started to learn Persian; there is absolutely no need for many of the convoluted linguistic rules you will encounter in many other grammar books:

تو از این کتاب خوشت می آید
tou az in ketaub khoshat mi auyad
you like this book

ما از تو خوشمان می آید
mau az tou khoshemaun mi auyad
we like you

مرد از آن ماشین خوشش نیامد
mard az aun maushin khoshash nayaumad
the man did not like that car

Like the other grammatical "tools" presented in this book, elevations can be used when learning any language. Using elevations both reduces the actual number of rules you have to learn and ensures you will never again have to learn convoluted rules for the more complex structures of that language. The remainder of this chapter is essentially a list of example elevations for you to learn; as in Chapter Three, this list is by no means exhaustive. Although I have given a very basic explanation of each elevation, you should study primarily the example itself. Look for the underlying literal structure and apply the rules you have learned; there is no need to formulate new rules.

"have seen"

To say "have seen", add the helper "...e" to the second form of an action and use this with "baush \ bud", as follows. In this instance, "hast" is always omitted:

من دیده ام
*man dide **am***
I have seen

من دیده بودم
*man dide **bud**am*
I had seen

To say "have not seen", add the helper "na...", as follows:

من ندیده ام
*man **na**dide am*
I have not seen

من ندیده بودم
*man **na**dide budam*
I had not seen

"will see"

To say "will see", use the helper "khauh" with the second form of an action. The helpers that added to the end of an action are added instead to "khauh", as follows:

من خواهم دید
*man **khauham** did*
I will see

ما خواهیم دید
*mau **khauhim** did*
we will see

To say "will not see", add the helper "*na...*", as follows:

من نخواهم ديد
*man **na**khauham did*
I will not see

ما نخواهيم ديد
*mau **na**khauhim did*
we will not see

"might see"

To say "might see", use the helper "*be...*" with the first form of an action, together with the helper "*shauyad*", as follows:

من شايد آن را ببينم
*man **shauyad** aun rau **be**binam*
I might see it

To say "might not see", use the helper "*na...*" instead of "*be...*":

من شايد آن را نبينم
*man **shauyad** aun rau **na**binam*
I might not see it

This is one of those situations mentioned in Chapter One, in which the helpers "*be...*" and "*na...*" are used with the first form of an action; there are several more below.

"can see"

To say "can see" or "is able to see", use the action "*tavaun \ tavaunest*" with another action, as follows:

من می توانم آن را ببینم

*man mi **tavaun**am aun rau **be**binam*
I can see it / I am able to see it

To say "cannot see" or "is not able to see", make the action "*tavaun \ tavaunest*" negative:

من نمی توانم آن را ببینم

*man **na**mi tavaunam aun rau bebinam*
I can not see it / I am not able to see it

Note also the following phrases:

من می توانستم آن را ببینم

*man **mi** tavaunestam aun rau bebinam*
I could see it / I was able to see it

من نمی توانستم آن را ببینم

*man **na**mi tavaunestam aun rau bebinam*
I could not see it / I was not able to see it

"must see"

To say "must see", use the helper *"bauyad"* with an action, as follows:

من باید آن را ببینم
*man **bauyad** aun rau **be**binam*
I must see it

To say "must not see", add the helper *"na..."*, as follows:

من نباید آن را ببینم
*man **na**bauyad aun rau **be**binam*
I must not see it

"should see"

To say "should see", use the helper *"bauyest"* in exactly the same way that *"bauyad"* is used to denote "must see":

من بایست آن را ببینم
*man **bauyest** aun rau **be**binam*
I should see it

من نبایست آن را ببینم
*man **na**bauyest aun rau **be**binam*
I should not see it

"be seen"

To say "be seen", add the helper "...e" to the second form of an action (as we did with "have seen") and use this with the action "shav \ shod", as follows:

من دیده شدم
man dide shodam
I am seen

من دیده شده ام
man dide shode am
I was seen

من دیده شده ام
man dide shode am
I have been seen

من دیده شده بودم
man dide shode budam
I had been seen

To say "is not seen", make the action "shav \ shod" negative (and not the action that takes "...e", as in the case of "have seen"):

من دیده نشدم
man dide nashodam
I am not seen

من دیده نشده ام
man dide nashode am
I was not seen

من دیده نشده ام
man dide nashode am
I have not been seen

من دیده نّشده بودم
man dide nashode budam
I had not been see

"to see"

To say "to see", connect two phrases with the helper "*ke*", as follows:

او می آید که آن را ببیند

*u mi auyad **ke** aun rau **be**binad*

he comes to see it

او می خواهد که آن را ببیند

*u mi khauhad **ke** aun rau **be**binad*

he wants to see it

This situation is simple enough; however, it is one of the many situations in Persian that have been complicated by well-meaning authors who insist on using grammatical conventions that do not, in fact, fit Persian. This doesn't just occur with Persian of course; it occurs with the grammatical descriptions of many languages. Other authors will tell you that to say "to see" in Persian, all you need to do is add the helper "...*an*" to the second form of an action. Of course, they won't use these labels; they will say you should start with an "infinitive" form ending in "...*an*", but let's ignore that for the moment and follow their advice:

بین \ دید

bin \ did

see

دیدن

*did**an***

to see

In my opinion, saying that *"didan"* denotes "to see" is very misleading. This is because "to see" is not usually translated like this; instead, as we have seen, a simple construction with *"ke"* is used. Equally, adding the helper *"...an"* to the end of the second form of an action does not in fact make an action at all—it creates an object. In theory, this object denotes "seeing", by which I mean "the action of seeing":

بین \ دید
bin \ did
see

دیدن
*did**an***
(the action of) seeing

This object is used just like any other:

نوشتن آسان هست
neveshtan *ausaun hast*
writing is easy

خواندن سختتر هست
khaundan *sachttar hast*
reading is harder

However, words for "seeing", "writing", "reading", etc often already exist; therefore, if you encounter a word that means "the action of seeing", it is probably easier simply to learn this word as an object in its own right (whether you consider this an "infinitive" ending in *"...an"* or not). In any event, you certainly should not start with the "infinitive" form when you learn actions. I have read page after page of needless rules about how "infinitives", "present stems", and "imperfect stems" are formed in Persian; the pressure to conform to traditional grammatical conventions is so strong that it does not occur to the authors of these resources that taking as a starting point what is in fact an ill-translated object and forcing the naïve learner to learn and apply acrobatic rules about how to form the "present stem" from that object is not the best way to learn about actions in Persian!   Even if you did learn every single "infinitive" form in Persian, you would still have very little idea (for any given "infinitve") what the first form of that action would be. In my view, the most efficient way of learning what in other books may be called the "present stem" and the "past stem" (if these two crucial bits of information are identified at all) is by simply learning the "present stem" and the "past stem"—otherwise known as the "first form" and "second form". When you are using resources to continue to improve your Persian, just ignore anything you read about "infinitives". For any given action, just find the first form and the second form.

"the man who"

To say "the man who", the helper *"ke"* is used to refer to a previous object, just as in English. The helper *"...i"* can be also be used to further specify an object, as follows:

مرد که دیروز آمد

*mard **ke** diruz aumad*
the man, who came yesterday ~who happened to come

مردی که دیروز آمد

*mardi **ke** diruz aumad*
the man who came yesterday ~and no other

Also, note phrases like the following:

مردی که من به او نامه را دادم

*mardi ke man be **u** naume rau daudam*

the man to whom I gave the letter

ماشینی که در آن زن می نشیند

maushini ke dar aun zan mi neshinad

the car in which the woman is sitting

Phrases with "*agar*"

For phrases with the helper "*agar*" — "if", observe the following changes to actions:

اگر من ببینم

*agar man **be**binam*

if I see

اگر من آن را می دیدم می رفتم

*agar man aun rau **mi did**am man **mi raft**am*

if I saw it, I would go

اگر من آن را می دیدم من می رفتم

*agar man aun rau **mi did**am man **mi raft**am*

if I had seen it, I would have gone

Actions denoted by phrases

In English, most actual actions are indicated by one word: "see", "go", "run", "eat", etc. Many actions in Persian are also denoted by one word (or two words, if you count both forms):

رو \ رفت

rav \ raft

go

بین \ دید

bin \ did

see

However, a huge number of actions in Persian are actually denoted by a whole phrase:

او یاد می گیرد

u yaud mi girad

he learns

او جواب می دهد

u javaub mi dehad

he answers

In phrases like these, an action appears with an additional word. Do not worry about the meaning of this additional word or what category of word it belongs to; you just need to learn the meaning of the phrase as a whole. Some more phrases that can be translated by a single action in English are listed below:

او جواب می دهد

u javaub mi dehad

he answers

او قبول می کند

u qabul mi konad

he accepts

او از من سوال می کند
u az man soaul mi konad
he asks me

او یقین دارد
u yaqin daurad
he is certain

او باور می کند
u bauvar mi konad
he believes

او قرض می کند
u qarzz mi konad
he borrows

او گپ می زند
u gap mi zanad
he chats

او انتخاب می کند
u entechaub mi konad
he chooses

او شکایت می کند
u shekauyat mi konad
he complains

او تصمیم می گیرد
u tassmim mi girad
he decides

او پیدا می کند
u peidau mi konad
he finds

او فراموش می کند
u faraumush mi konad
he forgets

و به من کمک می کند
u be man komak mi konad
he helps me

او امیدوار هست
u omidvaur hast
he hopes

او عجله می کند
u ájale mi konad
he hurries

آن درد می کند
aun dard mi konad
it hurts

او دعوت می کند
u dajhvat mi konad
he invites

او فارسی بلد هست
u Faursi balad hast
he knows Persian

او یاد می گیرد
u yaud mi girad
he learns

او دروغ می گوید
u dorugh mi guyad
he lies ~tells a lie

او گوش می دهد
u gush mi dehad
he listens

او زندگی می کند
u zendegi mi konad
he lives ~dwells

او دوست دارد
u dust daurad
he loves

او باز می کند
u bauz mi konad
he opens

او بازی می کند
u bauzi mi konad
he plays

او تمرین می کند
u tamrin mi konad
he practises

او ترجیح می دهد
u tarjihh mi dehad
he prefers

او قول می دهد
u qoul mi dehad
he promises

او تکرار می کند
u tekraur mi konad
he repeats

او استراحت می کند
u esterauhhat mi konad
he rests

او نشان می دهد

u neshaun mi dehad

he shows

او با من صحبت می کند

u bau man sóhhbat mi konad

he speaks to me

او درس می خواند

u dars mi khaunad

he studies

او پیشنهاد می کند

u pishnehaud mi konad

he suggests

او حرف می زند

u hárf mi zanad

he talks

او فکر می کند

u fekr mi konad

he thinks

او پیاده می رود

u piaude mi ravad

he walks

او نگاه می کند

u negauh mi konad

he watches

You may have noticed the word *"kon"* in the above examples; this is the first form of the action *"kon \ kard"* and is used in many phrases that denote actions. Be aware that other grammar books will tell you this action means *"do"*. This is a little misleading because the action *"do"* is more properly translated in Persian by a phrase of the type we have just looked at, which denotes *"work"*:

او کار می کند

u kaur mi konad

he does

او کار می کند

u kaur mi konad

he works

You will almost never hear the action "*kon \ kard*" by itself; it will usually be part of phrases like the ones above. If this action ever does appear by itself, it may be being used with an impolite meaning. For these reasons, in my opinion, it is easier to consider "*kon \ kard*" as an essentially meaningless action and one that is only used in elevations of the type we have looked at in this section. Traditional grammatical descriptons of languages are often reluctant to describe words as "meaningless", hence the insistence that "*kon \ kard*" actually means "do". It doesn't. If you try to use it with that meaning, then I can tell you from experience that you may find yourself in some embarrassing situations! Finally, note that when "*kon \ kard*" appears in phrases like the ones above, remove the helper "*be...*":

من بايد كار كنم

man bauyad kaur ~~be~~konam

I must work

Likewise, remove the whole action in the elevation that denotes "is seen":

او نشان مى دهد	آن نشان داده شد
u neshaun mi dehad	*aun neshaun daude shod*
he shows	it is shown
او تكرار مى كند	آن تكرار شد
u tekraur mi konad	*aun tekraur ~~karde~~ shod*
he repeats	it is repeated

Different doers

The following phrases are like the example discussed at the beginning of the chapter ("*man az ketaub khosham mi auyad*" – "I from the book my '*khosh*' comes"); essentially, the person who is performing the action in English is not the same as the person who is performing the action in the equivalent Persian phrase. Take a look at the following example:

من خوابم می برد
man khaubam mi barad
I fall asleep

Although the person who is performing the action appears ("*man*" – "I"), the action ends with the helper "*...ad*" (when we might otherwise expect it to end in "*...am*"); therefore, something other than "*man*" must be performing the action.   The answer is "*khaubam*" – "my sleep"; literally, you say "I my sleep carries":

ما خوابمان می برد
mau khaubemaun mi barad
we fall asleep

مردها خوابشان برد
mardhau khaubeshaun bord
the men fell asleep

Persian has a lot of phrases like this; there are several listed below for you to learn:

من یادم می رود
man yaudam mi ravad
I forget

من یادم هست
man yaudam hast
I remember

چند سالت هست؟   من سردم هست

Cand saulat hast?   *man sardam hast*

How old are you?   I am cold

من از کتاب خوشم می آید

man az ketaub khosham mi auyad

I like the book

من از کتاب بدم می آید

man az ketaub badam mi auyad

I dislike the book

Giving instructions

In order to tell someone to do something, use the first form of an action with the helper "*be...*", as follows:

غذا را بخور   کتاب را بخوان

ghaxau rau **bekhor**   *ketaub rau* **bekhaun**

eat the food   read the book

If you are talking to more than one person, add the helper "*...id*":

غذا را بخورید   کتاب را بخوانید

ghaxau rau **bekhorid**   *ketaub rau* **bekhaunid**

eat the food   read the book

Note that if the first form ends in the letters *AV*, change these letters to *O* (but not when "*...id*" is added):

به خانه برو
*be chaune ber**o***
go to the house

به خانه بروید
be chaune beravid
go to the house

To tell someone not to do something, simply use the helper "*na...*" instead of "*be...*" in all instances:

کتاب را نخوان
*ketaub rau **na**khaun*
don't read the book

غذا را نخورید
*ghaxau rau **na**khorid*
don't eat the food

به خانه نرو
*be chaune **na**ro*
don't go to the house

به خانه نروید
*be chaune **na**ravid*
don't go to the house

Showing respect

In Persian, there is a very specific way you can show respect through language; this involves simply referring to a person as if he or she were a group of people:

مرد ایجا هست
mard injau hast
the man is here

مرد اینجا هستند
*mard injau hast**and***
the man is here ~respectful

تو اینجا هستی   شما اینجا هستید

tou injau hasti   **shomau** *injau hast**id***

you are here   you are here ~respectful

In addition, the object "*u*" becomes "*ishaun*":

او ایجا هست   ایشان اینجا هستند

u injau hast   *ishaun injau hast**and***

he is here   he is here ~respectful

Other elevations

The following is a list of some other elevations that you may find useful. Where necessary, I have highlighted parts of the English or Persian translation that are especially important or which otherwise illustrate the crucil difference between the literal English and Persian meanings:

هشت لیوان آب   سه روز به سه روز

hasht livaun aub   *se ruz be se ruz*

eight glasses **of** water   every three days

او بیست سال دارد   من گفتم که من می آیم

*u bist saul **daurad***   *man goftam ke man **mi auy**am*

he **is** twenty years old   I said I **was** coming

مرد هست

mard hast

there is the man

مردان هستند

mardaun hastand

there are men

ساعت چند هست؟

Saujhat cand hast?

What time is it?

ساعت پنج هست

saujhat-e-panj hast

it's five o'clock

من گفتم که من خواهم آمد

*man goftam ke man **khauh**am **aumad***

I said I **would** come

دو روز هست که او آن را می نویسد

dou ruz hast ke u aun rau mi nevisad

he has been writing it for two days

خیلی ممنونم از این کتاب

kheili mamnunam az in ketaub

thank you for this book

تو ... به فارسی چی می گویی؟

*Tou ... be Faursi **ci** mi guyi?*

How do you say ... in Persian?

Of course, there are many more elevations you will need to learn. As you may have guessed from the examples in this section, it is often the case that some of the most frequently used phrases in a language can be quite complex elevations. If you only ever learn lots of abstract rules and memorise lots of words, you will be able to say a huge number of phrases; however, when you start to learn elevations and subsequently use them, you really begin to "use" the language in the proper sense of the word because you will be manipulating both abstract rules and words at the same time. For the technically minded, imagine that your mouth and ears are the basic "hardware" you use to produce and understand a language, the rules you have been learning are the "operating system" of that language, and the words of the language are your "files". In this analogy, elevations are the "software" you use to actually do anything but the most basic tasks; elevations are fundamental when producing and understanding any language.

Chapter Five: Intermediate Rules

Now that we have discussed the basic and elementary rules of Persian, including "grammatical" rules in the traditional sense, rules about pronunciation, and the words and elevations in the previous two chapters, we are ready to look at the more intermediate rules of Persian. In many ways, these rules can quite happily be separated from the rest of the rules in this book, since they are concerned with only two quite isolated aspects of Persian: the script and the differences between spoken and written Persian.

Persian script

There is no denying that Persian script poses some very specific challenges for many learners. Of course, learning a completely different script for any language poses significant challenges; whereas Spanish, Italian, and German for example are in many ways easier for an English speaker to learn because they have pretty much the same script as English (albeit with minor differences), languages like Hindi, Greek, and Russian have completely different scripts from English and in this respect would probably be harder for an English speaker to learn. Nevertheless, in my opinion, the challenges posed by Persian script are greater than those posed by the scripts used for Hindi, Greek, or Russian.

This is because (as mentioned in Chapter One) Persian script does not for the most part represent vowels—at least, the learner may often be unsure whether some of the symbols used to represent vowels actually do represent vowels or not. Even Arabic- and Urdu-speaking learners, who share the same script as Persian, still have the same basic problem as English-speaking learners: when you encounter a new word, you can never be completely sure how that word is pronounced. This is not the case with other scripts that do represent all (or at least more) of the sounds of a given word, such as English and French (however inconsistently), Greek, Spanish, and Russian (regularly), and Hindi (which has a very systematic and logical writing system). Of course, you could argue that learners of English face a similar situation, since English spelling can be quite "unique" at times; even native English speakers are often not entirely sure how they should pronounce many less-frequent words (particularly place names). Equally, you could argue that you don't actually need all the vowels in a given word or phrase to read and understand it in the first place:

if yu cn red ths yu shld undrstnd wht I men

Here, we don't need all the vowels because we are already native speakers of the language and can therefore "fill in the blanks". As learners of Persian, we are not yet able to instantly sift through all the possible combinations of words that might fit, while bearing in mind context and genre, which literate native speakers of a language do automatically and effortlessly. Of course, the issue with Persian is further compounded because a learner is expected to do this with almost every single word. Encountering new words in Persian that are written in "vowel-less" Persian script and actually trying to learn them in that script is a bit like trying to learn

English words from a dictionary in which all the entries appear without vowels:

ct	*v. to perform*
ct	*n. a small feline animal*
ct	*v. to reference an author*
ct	*n. a baby's bed*
ct	*v. to shear or separate with a blade*
ct	*a. pretty or lovely*

Admittedly, this is a slight exaggeration because not all vowels in Persian are unwritten; yet, if you have never before tried to learn Persian words written solely in Persian script, then this example does give you a taste of how frustrating it can be to use some Persian dictionaries. (I have seen dictionaries and even whole grammars and coursebooks of Arabic-script languages, in which the entries and the supposedly illustrative examples are in "vowel-less" Arabic script, and it's all utterly pointless from the learner's perspective.) Of course, this does not mean to say that the scripts used to write languages like English, Hindi, Greek, or Russian are any "better" than the scripts used to write Arabic, Persian, or Urdu. In fact, you could argue that the latter use a script that is in many ways far more efficient because you neither have to use as many little symbols to represent individual sounds nor decode as many of those symbols when reading. Equally, as mentioned above, there is a system in Arabic, Persian, and Urdu that allows the writer to represent the vowels of a given word, albeit one that is not normally used in most texts.

Leaving Persian script till last

This is the reason why Persian script is discussed in this book in this last main chapter and not the first. Many books and classes on Persian begin with a discussion of the script; in my view, this is a more difficult way of progressing than approaching the script after you have learned both lots of words and how the language is actually structured. The simple reason for this is that you now have the advantage (just as a native-speaking child does) of already knowing lots of words in Persian; therefore, when you do encounter written words, you might be able to take a good guess at what word is denoted since you already have a "bank" of those words in your brain. Nobody would expect children to learn how to read words in their first language before they can actually speak that language to the level they are able to speak it when they first start school and begin to learn to read and write; therefore, why expect adults to do this?

There might be an argument for learning the script before you learn anything else if the script you are learning is "phonetic" enough (like Greek, Hindi, or Russian) that it represents the sounds of a given word to the extent that the reader can pronounce that word fairly confidently; however, the simple fact is that Persian does not. You are also at the stage now where you don't need to worry about both rules and the script at the same time; because the rules you have learned have already been "mapped" in your brain using the letters of the English alphabet, it is now a much smaller step to subsequently see them in action in Persian script. In my view, if you were decoding the script at the same time as using the script to illustrate grammatical rules, you would be faced with a much steeper learning curve. Therefore, with all this in mind, let's now look at how to form words in Persian script.

Shapes

Arabic script (and its derivatives Persian and Urdu script) is one in which letters are joined together in almost the same way that "cursive" letters in English are joined together. The traditional way of learning Arabic script is similar to the way you probably learned how to produce "joined-up" writing at school—albeit a lot less efficient! The traditional way involves laboriously memorising what each letter looks like when it is joined to the letter to its left, joined to the letter to its right, joined on both sides, and joined on neither side. In my view, memorising different forms for what are essentially manifestations of the same underlying shape is just like learning all the possible forms of different cursive letters in handwritten English: extremely inefficient. The disadvantage of having a long history of linguistic analysis is that traditions become cemented; it seems to me that Arabic, Persian, and Urdu script are taught this way because this is "the way things have always been done". In my view, it is intuitively easier to simply learn the basic, underlying form of a letter together with the point on that letter that it joins to the previous letter. In other words, for each letter, you learn one basic shape. This sounds complicated, but it is probably just like you learned how to write cursively at school. And the good news is there is only a very limited set of these basic shapes; in fact, there are only five! Almost all the letters of Persian script are all variations on this set of underlying and fundamental *shapes*:

ا ص ح س م

A shape is joined to the following shape along the line of writing. By "following" shape, I mean of course the shape to the left, since Persian script runs from right to left:

لصحسمسحصد

At the end of a word, shapes take a final "flourish"; let's call these final flourishes *tails*:

ب ص ح س م

Think of these forms a little like capital letters in English, except that they appear at the end of every word:

مس حص سحب

These forms also help to distinguish between individual words in Persian texts, especially since words are often written very close together (at least in comparison to English); you can assume that any instance of a letter with a flourish like this indicates the end of a word.

Letters

As I mentioned, these basic shapes are used to form the *letters* of Persian script. Only three shapes have a one-to-one correspondence with some English letters used in this book:

د	سـ	مـ
D	*S*	*M*

Most other shapes require the addition of dots, lines, extensions, or loops (or combinations thereof) to form other letters. The first shape in our original bank of shapes is the most productive and takes a variety of these additions to denote various letters:

نـ	تـ	بـ	یـ	پـ
N	*T*	*B*	*Y*	*P*

لـ	ک	گ	ف	ق
L	*K*	*G*	*F*	*Q*

The following shape takes dots to denote letters:

جـ   چ

J   *C*

The letter combinations used in this book are formed from the following shapes and additions:

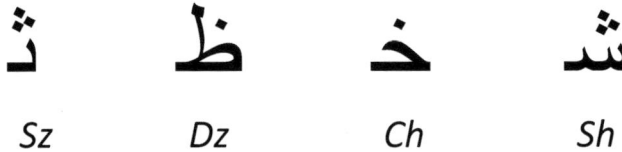

ثـ   ظـ   خـ   شـ

Sz   *Dz*   *Ch*   *Sh*

Finally, note that any instance of a doubled *S, Z, T,* or *H* in this book is also formed by the following shapes and additions:

صـ   ضـ   طـ   حـ

SS   *ZZ*   *TT*   *HH*

This is the basic system for writing in Persian script. There are of course some additional rules that apply, and these are discussed in the sections below. Note that the examples used will manifest features of the script you have not yet learned; as you work through, simply focus on the relevant part of the example only.

Consonants

Many changes occur with the first and most productive shape in our original bank of shapes; when this shape appears with a tail, any accompanying dots appear above the centre of that tail:

پوست

pust

skin

جیب

jib

pocket

This does not occur with the letters *F* and *Q*:

کیف

kif

bag

اتاق

otauq

room

As you can see, the tail dips below the line of writing in the case of *Q*; this also occurs when the shape is used to denote *N* and *L*:

سن

sen

age

هتل

hotel

hotel

With the letter *D*, the shape is not joined, and there is no tail:

مدیر

modir

manager

مسجد

masjed

mosque

Adding a dot to this shape denotes the letter *X*, as follows:

كاغذ

kaughax

paper

دلپذیر

delpaxir

nice

The same unjoined shape is used for *R*, but in this case, the shape dips below the line of writing, as follows:

ترسیده

tarside

afraid

دختر

dochtar

daughter

Likewise, adding a dot to this shape denotes the letter *Z*; adding three dots denotes the letter combination *Zh*:

ژاکت

zhaukat

jacket

زیبا

zibau

beautiful

Adding a loop to this shape denotes the letter *V*:

ورزش

varzesh

sport

مسواک

mesvauk

toothbrush

The letter *H* is denoted by a series of unique shapes; at the end of a word, it looks like the head of a cat in profile, as follows:

نه

nah

no

نه

noh

nine

After a shape that does not join, it looks like a teardrop:

ده

dah

ten

ماه

mauh

month

In all other positions, the letter *H* looks like an eye or a bow tied in a ribbon, depending on whether it is joined to the previous letter:

هست

hast

is

چهار

cahaur

fou

The underlying shape that is used to denote *HH* also denotes the letter combinations *Jh* and *Gh* (with the latter taking a dot); however, in this instance, the shape curve upwards instead of downwards, as follows:

به سرعت

be sorjhat

about

مرغ

morgh

chicken

When it is joined to the previous letter, the shape curves all the way around to form a loop, as follows:

راجع به
raujejh be
about

شغل
shoghl
job

When appearing at the beginning of a word, the letter combination *Jh* is not written; instead, the following vowel appears with a mark, as follows:

عراق
Érauq
Iraq

عربی
Árabi
Arabic

It may seem counterintuitive to use a conspicuous letter combination like *Jh* to represent a Persian script letter that is not even pronounced in Persian (in most instances). Many other resources for Persian do not represent this letter at all or represent it using an apostrophe. Not representing this letter is of course problematic because there would be no way of knowing (beyond learning the script right from the beginning) which words contained this letter and which did not, and the letter proliferates the Persian lexicon enough to make learning isolated examples impossible. Equally, using an apostrophe to represent this letter looks (to me) distorted and unnatural. The script used in this book to represent Persian using the letters of the English alphabet was designed to be a viable script in its own right, and so an aberrant apostrophe was not really an option. In my opinion, it is the fact that *Jh* is conspicuous that allows the reader to ignore it all the more effectively. English speakers have learned to automatically ignore the letters GH in words like "though" for example, and I believe they would find ignoring a similar combination like *Jh* easier than being distracted by a more covert, but unfamiliarly placed, apostrophe. The following minor changes also reflect this aim. If the letters *H, S,* or *Z* appear before a vowel that has a mark above it, they are written as if they were *HH, SS,* and *ZZ* respectively; likewise, *Dt* was chosen as an alternative to *TT* in order to reduce the instances of vowels with marks (which are more difficult to write using online media):

حسود

hásud

jealous

صندلى

sándali

chair

ضعيف

zájhif

weak

طبقه

dtabaqe

floor

There are two final changes that occur. The letter combination *Kh* is written as *Ch* followed by *V*, and at the end of a word, *NN* is written as if it was *Au* (see the next section) but with two parallel lines above it:

خودكار

khodkaur

pen

لطفاً

lottfann

please

Vowels

As you will have noticed by now, none of the basic shapes used in Persian script represents the vowels *A*, *E*, or *O*; for the most part, these vowels are left unwritten:

مرد

mard

man

کتاب

ketaub

book

خشک

chosk

book

تلفن

telefon

telephone

However, at the end of a word, *E* is written as if it were *H*:

گربه

gorbe

cat

ستاره

setaure

star

The other vowels—*Au*, *I*, and *U*—are denoted by shapes that are otherwise used for consonants. First, the shape that denotes *L* is used for *Au*; in this instance, the shape is not joined to the following shape, and no tail appears:

لهستان

Lahestaun

Poland

سال

saul

year

The shape that denotes *Y* is used for *I*:

قیمت

qeimat

price

سفید

sefid

white

At the end of a word—whether it is denoting *Y* or *I*—this shape appears in a different form; again, note the slight difference between the joined and the unjoined forms:

آبی

aubi

blue

فرانسوی

Faraunsavi

French

The shape that denotes *V* is used for *U*:

پوست

pust

skin

روشن

roushan

light

This shape is also used for *O*, but only at the end of a word; note that I have not done this in the case of the two common words "*tou*" and "*dou*" in order to avoid mispronunciations based on the English words "to" and "do" respectively:

پلو

polo

rice

تو

tou

you

It is important to note that if a word begins with any vowel, then you must write that word as if it began with *Au*. This is the only feature that makes it possible to distinguish whether the shapes for *L*, *Y*, and *V* are being used to denote vowels or consonants:

انگلستان

Englestaun
England

ایران

Iraun
Iran

If the word already begins with *Au*, an additional curved mark appears, as follows:

آب

aub
water

آقا

auqau
sir

Finally, note that the helper "-*e*-" is not usually written (which makes sense, given that it is the letter *E*):

کتاب بزرگ

ketaub-e-bozorg
the big book

مرد جوان

mard-e-javaun
my book

However, after a word that ends in a vowel, it is written as *Y*:

کتابهای بزرگ

ketaubhau-e-bozorg
the big books

گربه ی من

gorbe-e-man
my book

Other shapes

In addition to letters, there are three additional sets of symbols that are used in Persian script; these are symbols for the vowels *A*, *E*, and *O*, numbers, and punctuation. As discussed earlier in this chapter, the sounds *A*, *E*, and *O* are not written in Persian script; however, there is a system that can be used to represent these letters which uses additional symbols. In practice, these symbols are only used to clarify the pronunciation of words. They are usually not written in any type of text; even in texts written for children, they are often inconsistently applied. This is because (as discussed in Chapter One) Persian speakers already know most of the words they will encounter, and they know how to pronounce them; therefore, Persian speakers are able to effortlessly "sift" through all the possible combinations of potential words that might fit. This system can be a useful way of receiving written clarification about the pronunciation of new words in Persian script, but the problem is very few written resources actually use this system—even dictionaries! As I mentioned in Chapter One, be wary of resources that are billed "for learners"; often, they use neither this system nor English letters for much-needed clarification of pronunciation. The system itself is actually very straightforward; the following three symbols denote that *A*, *E*, or *O* appear after the letter beneath them:

مَرد

mard

man

كِتاب

ketaub

book

نُه

noh

nine

تِلِفُن

telefon

telephone

The following symbol denotes that there is no vowel after the letter beneath it:

مرْد

mard

man

چنْگال

cangaul

fork

The following symbol denotes that the consonant beneath it is pronounced longer:

بچّه

bace

child

اوّل

aval

first

In many resources, letters that appear with this symbol are often represented by doubling the corresponding English letter. I have not done this in this book because these additional symbols are not usually written, doubled letters have already been used in this book to represent certain shapes, and representing a consonant that is pronounced longer as a doubled consonant is inherently misleading. Persian belongs to the same language "family" as English, and in languages of this family, it is often not so crucial to pronounce a consonant longer (unlike vowels, which usually do have very clearly defined longer and shorter versions). You would not usually be misunderstood in English, at least when speaking at normal speed, if you pronounce the word "midday" as "mi-day" for instance. In other languages, including Arabic (from which Persian took its script and a lot of vocabulary), it is actually very important to pronounce some consonants longer, and you may be misunderstood if you do not; in Persian, unless you are saying the word individually, you are extremely unlikely to be misunderstood if you do not pronounce a consonant like this longer. Contrary to what many learners think at first, Persian is a very different language from Arabic, and longer consonants are not an integral part of it. The point at which these letters may even become the slightest issue for you is the point at which your fluency in reading and speaking will be such that it would only be a very minor improvement to methodically pronounce them longer anyway! Another symbol you will sometimes encounter is the symbol ء; this usually appears "resting" on top of other shapes:

ژوئن
Zhuan
June

ژوئیه
Zhuie
July

This symbol is often used in words of English or French origin to denote that two vowels come together (as in the examples above) or in the spelling of words of Arabic origin (since in Arabic, this symbol used to represent a consonant). In my view, as opposed to learning complex rules, it is much simpler just to learn where this symbol goes in individual words, especially since the number of words containing it is limited. Note that after a word ending in the letter *E*, the helper "*-e-*" used to be denoted by this symbol, and you may also still encounter this symbol as a replacement for the *Y* of the letters *YI*; neither of these uses usually occurs in modern texts:

گربهٔ سیاه
*gorbe-**e**-siauh*
the black cat

پائیز
pauyiz
autumn

The following symbols are used to denote numbers:

۱	۲	۳	۴	۵
1	2	3	4	5

۶	۷	۸	۹	۰
6	7	8	9	0

Note that numbers are written from left to right, as in English:

۱۸۹۲
1892
1892

۲۵۵ سیب
255 sib
255 apples

Punctuation symbols are usually the same as in English, except that they are written reversed (as you might expect); commas are also inverted:

آیا تو می روی؟
Auyau tou mi ravi?
Do you go?

آب، شیر، شراب.
Aub, shir, sharaub.
Water, milk, wine.

Spoken and written Persian

To a certain extent, different rules are used in Persian depending on whether you are speaking or writing. This may seem a little strange, but we actually have a similar situation in English. Imagine you are writing an essay for school or college; most likely, you are not going to use the same kind of language you would use when speaking. Instead of saying "wanna", "woulda", or "gonna" etc, you would write "want to", "would have", and "going to" etc. The same principle applies in Persian; when you are speaking, you use slightly different rules from when you are writing. The rules you have learned so far in this book are—more or less—the rules of *written* Persian. The rules in this section are the rules of *spoken* Persian. When speaking, if you continue to use the rules you have learned so far, you will be completely understood, but your Persian will sound very stilted and formal; when speaking Persian, try at least to use some of the rules in this section.

This is not as big a task as you might expect because the "new" rules of spoken Persian are all simple modifications to the existing rules you already know, and as you will be hearing them in action all the time, these changes very soon become automatic (to the extent that you then have to consciously try not to use them). Esssentially, these rules are the "standard" rules of modern Persian; as with English spelling, it is only because Persian has a rich literary history that these changes have not been incorporated into the written language (because written language is recorded in a "permanent" form, it is usually more conservative than the spoken language). That said, you will sometimes encounter the modifications discussed in this section in written Persian, for example in personal emails or notes between friends etc. Likewise, you will sometimes not encounter these modifications in spoken Persian, for example in speeches or formal debates etc.

This is because the differences between spoken and written Persian are actually the differences between informal and formal Persian. It is just easier to refer to "spoken" and "written" Persian because it just so happens that most of the things you will read and write are essentially formal (application forms, books, newspapers, professional documents, public signs, etc) and most of the things you will hear or say are essentially informal (compare the number of times in your life you have given a speech with the number of times you've chatted with your friends). Therefore, it is much more convenient not to think of the informal-versus-formal distinction at all; when you are speaking Persian, simply use the rules you have learned so far, but apply the modifications in this section. Similarly, if you are writing something to your friend, just write as you would speak.

Changes to letters

In spoken Persian, the letter combination *Au*, when followed by the letter *N*, is pronounced as the letter *U*:

جوون
javun
young

اونها
unhau
they

Therefore, the object *"aun"* becomes *"un"*; the object *"u"* also appears as *"un"* in spoken Persian:

اون رفت
un raft
it went

اون دید
un did
he saw

When speaking at normal speed, the letters *H* and *Y* are often not really pronounced; however, they are still pronounced as normal at the beginning of a word (English speakers would probably do this anyway, at least in the case of *H*):

مردا

mardau

men

ما

mau

month

Any surrounding vowels combine into one, as follows:

کتابام

ketaubaum

my books

میاد

miaud

he comes

The letters *AR* at the end of the words *"agar"*, *"digar"*, and the associated *"hamdigar"* and *"yekdigar"* are pronounced as *E*:

اگه

age

if

دیگه

dige

other

همدیگه

hamdige

each other

یکدیه

yekdige

each other

Changes to objects

Objects in spoken Persian are omitted when their identity is obvious (which is often due to the helper attached to an action):

ﻣﯿﺒﯿﻨﻢ
*mibin**am***
I see

ﻣﯿﺒﯿﻨﯿﻢ
*mibin**im***
we see

When denoting "the book" instead of "book" etc, objects may also appear with the helper "...*e*":

ﮐﺘﺎﺑﻪ
*ketaub**e***
the book

ﭘﺴﺮﻩ
*pesar**e***
the boy

This helper is like "...*hau*" in that it becomes part of the word itself; being the last part, it is thus pronounced more strongly:

ﮐﺘﺎﺑﻪ
ketaube
"ketauBE"

ﭘﺴﺮﻩ
pesare
"pesaRE"

It is probably a good idea to avoid using this helper until you are more confident in Persian. Not all objects may be used like this; likewise, native speakers will not expect you to use it, and they may think you are trying to use the helper "-*e*-". For now, I would recommend that you just recognise this change when you encounter it but not attempt it yourself.

Changes to helpers

In spoken Persian, the helpers *"...ad"*, *"...and"*, and *"...id"* are pronounced *"...e"*, *"...an"*, and *"...in"* respectively:

میبینه

mibine

he sees

میخوره

mikhore

he eats

میبینن

mibinan

they see

میبینین

mibinin

you see

The shortened form *"ast"* is pronounced *"...e"*:

کتاب بزرگه

ketaub bozorge

the book is big

مرد جوونه

mard javune

the man is young

The helper *"rau"* is pronounced *"ro"*; after a consonant, this can become *"...o"*:

کشتی رو میبینه

keshti ro mibine

he sees the ship

کتابو میبینه

ketaubo mibine

he sees the book

The special combination *"marau"* may therefore revert to the more logical *"mano"*:

منو میبینه
mano mibine
he sees me

کتاب منو میبینه
ketaube mano mibine
he sees my book

The helpers *"nami"*, *"...ash"*, and *"...at"* are pronounced *"nemi"*, *"...esh"*, and *"...et"* respectively:

نمیبینه
nemibine
he does not see

نمیخورد
nemikhord
he did not eat

کتابش
ketaubesh
his book

کتابت
ketaubet
your book

The helpers *"...ash"*, *"...eshaun"*, *"...at"*, and *"...etaun"* may be attached to actions, replacing objects with *"rau"*, as follows:

میبینمش
mibinamesh
I see him

دیدمش
didamesh
I saw him

میبینمش
mibinamesh
I see it

میبینمشون
mibinameshun
I see them

میبینمتون
mibinametun
I see you

میبینمت
mibinamet
I see you

As mentioned in Chapter Four, some actual actions in Persian may be denoted by phrases:

او نشان می دهد
u neshaun mi dehad
he shows

او پیدا می کند
u peidau mi konad
he finds

In such phrases, helpers such as "...ash", "...eshaun", "...at", and "...etaun" are added to the extra word that appears before the action:

نشونت میده
neshunet mide
he shows you

او پیداش میکنه
u peidaush mikone
he shows you

The helper "auyau" is not used in spoken Persian; to make a question, a phrase is instead pronounced with a questioning intonation, just as in English we can form a question by saying "You're going home?" instead of "Are you going home?":

زنو دیدی؟
Zano didi?
Did you see the woman?

مرد میاد؟
Mard miaud?
Is the man coming?

The helper *"be..."* is pronounced *"bo..."* if the action to which it is attached contains the letter *O*:

<table>
<tr><td align="right">شاید بخوره</td><td align="right">شاید کار بکنه</td></tr>
<tr><td>shauyad bokhore</td><td>shauyad kaur bokone</td></tr>
<tr><td>he might eat</td><td>he might work</td></tr>
</table>

The following helpers and objects may combine into new forms:

از او		ازش
az u	>	*azesh*
از آن		ازش
az aun	>	*azesh*
از ایشان		ازشون
az ishaun	>	*azeshun*
به او		بهش / بش
be u	>	*behesh / besh*
به آن		بهش / بش
be aun	>	*behesh / besh*
به ایشان		بشون
be ishaun	>	*beshun*

به من   بهم
be man   >   *behem*

به تو   بهت
be tou   >   *behet*

Finally, the helper *"yek"* may be pronounced *"ye"* before a word beginning with a consonant:

یه کتاب   یه مرد
ye *ketaub*   **ye** *mard*
a book   a man

Note that an alternative way of saying "a man" or "a book" is to use the helper *"...i"*. This helper is more usually used in written Persian. I have not mentioned this helper until now because in my experience, if you attempt to use *"...i"* to denote "a" or "an", many native speakers may misinterpret what you are trying to say; partly, this is because you will most likely be having a conversation in an informal situation (and so you should be using *"ye"* to denote "a man" or "a book" etc anyway), but it is also because native speakers will be expecting you to make mistakes. This is particularly the case with *"...i"* because this helper is also used in a very specific elevation that has nothing to do with "a" or "an" (as described in Chapter Four):

مردی که من دیدم
mardi ke man didam
the man whom I saw

Changes to actions

In spoken Persian, the following actions all have different first forms, as follows:

ده \ داد *deh \ daud*	>	د \ د/اد **d** \ *daud*
گذر \ گذشت *goxar \ goxasht*	>	گذر \ گذشت **gxar** \ *goxasht*
گذار \ گذاشت *goxaur \ goxausht*	>	گذار \ گذاشت **gxaur** \ *goxausht*
گو \ گفت *gu \ goft*	>	گ \ گفت **g** \ *goft*
نشین \ نشست *neshin \ neshast*	>	شین \ نشست **shin** \ *neshast*
رو \ رفت *rav \ raft*	>	ر \ رفت **r** \ *raft*
شو \ شد *shav \ shod*	>	ش \ شد **sh** \ *shod*

The action "*tavaun \ tavaunest*" is different in both forms:

توان \ توانست	تون \ تونست
tavaun \ tavaunest >	**tun \ tunest**
be able	be able

All these forms are otherwise used as normal:

میده	میرم
mide	*miram*
he gives	I go

To say "I will see" etc, just say "I see"; the elevation with "*khauh*" is not used in spoken Persian:

میبینم	میرم
mibinam	*miram*
I will see	I will go

As mentioned in Chapter One, "I see" can also denote "I am seeing" etc; likewise, "I used to see" can also denote "I was seeing" etc:

من می بینم	ما نمی دیدیم
man mi binam	*mau nami didim*
I am seeing	we were not seeing

However, in spoken Persian, these phrases may be denoted by using the action "*daur \ dausht*", as follows:

دارم اون کتابو میخونم

***daur**am un ketaubo mikhunam*

I am reading that book

داشتم اون کتابو میخوندم

***dausht**am un ketaubo mikhundam*

I was reading that book

However, this does not occur for "not seeing":

كتابو نميخونم

ketaubo nemikhunam

I am not reading the book

كتابو نميخوندم

ketaubo nemikhundam

I was not reading the book

Finally, an object that denotes a location may appear after an action (and not before it, as would usually occur):

میرم لندن

*miram **Landan***

I go to London

بیا اینجا

*biau **injau***

come here

Typing Persian online

When writing Persian online, many speakers use the letters of the English alphabet instead of Persian script because it is still often difficult to write in certain scripts online. If you type Persian using the system of English letters used in this book, you should be understood well enough. However, it would be advisable to make the following changes to make it easier for Persian speakers to understand what you are trying to say. First, definitely do not type the letter combination *Jh*:

معلم

moalem

teacher

عربی

Arabi

Arabic

All variations of the letters *H, N, T, S,* and *Z* should not be used; likewise, vowels with marks should not be used:

بحرین

Bahrein

Bahrain

لطفاً

lotfan

please

صندلی

sandali

chair

ظرف

zarf

dish

Type the letter combination *Au* as "A". Note that you will find this use of the letter "A" to denote both *A* and *Au* a very frustrating feature of any written Persian (not just in informal typing). It compounds the tendency of learners to pronounce this sound as the short A of "cat" or the longer A of "father"; I've heard even advanced learners of Persian insist on pronouncing *Au* like this—despite the fact that *Au* represents a perfectly familiar sound that occurs in English: the AU of "author" or the AW of "dawn":

كتاب

ketab

book

شما دادید

shoma dadid

you gave

The letter *C* should be typed as "CH"; the combination *Ch* itself should always be typed as its counterpart *Kh*:

چهار فنجان چای

char fenjan chai

four cups of tea

این خانه خوب هست

in khane khub hast

this house is good

Similarly, the letter *Q* should be typed as its counterpart *Gh*:

قرمز

ghermez

red

جزیره قشنگ هست

jazire ghashang hast

the island is pretty

Finally, note that some Persian speakers type the letter *E* at the end of a word (including the helper "*-e-*") as "EH":

این مرد حسود

in mardeh hasud

this jealous man

جزیره قشنگ هست

jazireh ghashang hast

the island is beautiful

Some even imitate English spelling by typing "EE" and "OO" for the letters *I* and *U* respectively:

جزیره قشنگ هست

این مرد حسود

*ee*n mardeh has*oo*d

this jealous man

*jazee*reh ghashang hast

the island is beautiful

Conclusion

Congratulations on completing this book on Persian grammar. The question you might be asking yourself now is: "Where do I go from here?" There are many different theories about how best to study a language. In my view, they all involve at some point learning rules, words, and elevations and improving your speaking, listening, writing, and reading skills until you can understand and produce the language with your desired degree of ease (which is determined, of course, by how well you want to understand and produce that language). Hopefully, this section will give you some pointers about how to do that.

Where are the "advanced" rules?

The aim of this book was to develop your knowledge of Persian to the extent that you might never need to consult another grammar book again or even attend another formal Persian class. This is because you can classify anything you encounter in Persian from now on in terms of the rules you have learned; if you encounter a new word, you will be able to classify it as an object, helper, descriptor, or action, and you will know how to use it accordingly. Similarly, if you encounter a phrase that you cannot translate literally, you will know that you have encountered an elevation and that you need to learn a single example of it.

Just as you will encounter additional words and elevations, you will of course still encounter additional rules; there are some very specific rules about pronunciation that have not been mentioned in this book (for example, the few objects that are pronounced more strongly on the first part of the word or rules about the different Persian accents). Equally, there are more rules about Persian script (for example, all the unusual features of handwritten Persian). There are even more "grammatical" rules in the traditional sense of the word, though you will be able to classify most of these as elevations. I've called all these rules "advanced", and have not attempted to include them in this book.

Partly, this is because this book was written for the beginner and is not designed to be an encyclopedia of every single rule in the language; mostly though, I have not tried to include every single rule in Persian because the most important thing to remember about advanced rules is that you do not need to worry so much about them! The point at which you might want to take more notice of advanced rules that cover very specific details of technical grammatical points is the point at which you can deal with them perfectly well without either this book or any other grammar book! Although you now have a mental structure that you can use to organise any new information you encounter, if you subsequently hear or read something that sounds incredibly complex, just ignore it and don't come back to it until your Persian is at the level that someone would be able to explain it to you in Persian; in other words, so long as you understand the gist of the conversation you are having or the movie you are watching, everything is fine! Don't let a very specific little rule interrupt your Persian family dinner or the plot of your favourite Iranian soap opera.

Finally, remember that all the labels used in this book ("objects", "helpers", "actions", "descriptors", "rules", and "elevations") are merely mental tools to organise a language. They are very much arbitrary, and you should use them in a way that you think is the most appropriate—not necessarily in the way that I or any other author defines. For example, you might prefer to consider phrases such as *"posht-e-chaune"* – "behind the house" as an object (*"chaune"* – "house") with a helper (*"posht-e-"* – "behind"), as I have done:

[posht-e-]chaune > [behind] the house

However, you could equally consider phrases such as this as two objects (*"posht"* – "back" and *"chaune"* – "house") joined by a helper (*"-e-"*), producing an elevation (*"posht-e-chaune"* – "the back of the house", elevated to "behind the house"):

behind
posht-e-chaune > ~~the back of~~ the house

Either way is absolutely acceptable and fundamentally "correct". Despite what you might infer from other grammar books, there is no definitive analysis in grammar; simply use the "tools" that both best describe the phrase and best fit the language as a whole. If an analysis allows you to understand and produce correct phrases in any given language, then that analysis is itself just as correct as any found in a peer-reviewed journal.

What do I need to do now?

As I mentioned, you probably won't need to attend any more formal classes or read any more grammar books. What you definitely do need to do is learn more words and elevations, practise recognising and using the rules in this book, and practise your speaking, listening, writing, and reading skills. Fortunately, there is a very easy way to do all these things at the same time in a natural manner: simply do things in Persian! This may sound like a very obvious point, but I am often surprised at how even people who have learned languages before come to a weekly class and expect to improve when they neither attempt to speak Persian in that class nor do anything in Persian between classes. Of course, time is an issue for everyone, and it is much easier actually doing things in Persian if you have Iranian friends or family, have hours free to spend practising, or live in Iran etc. But whatever your situation, if you do want to learn a language, at some point you need to actually do things in that language.

So what do I mean by "doing things" in Persian? I am presuming that you do not live in Iran; if you do, the answer to this question should be obvious: you need to go outside and have conversations and read and write things! You certainly should not surround yourself in an English-speaking bubble, as many people living abroad still do. First, despite what I said before, don't quit your weekly Persian class or give away your grammar books. Use the time in class to actually have conversations in Persian—at least, as much as the teacher will allow. Remember that your teacher will probably still think it is his or her job to teach you grammar, though in the case of Persian, your teacher will probably be more concerned about teaching you the script. With Arabic-script languages generally, I have noticed a tendency for teachers to start with the script at all costs, as though the script were the ultimate key to the whole language. (The pressure to focus on the script seems so strong that I have seen Persian teachers persist in teaching Arabic script—to Arabic-speaking learners!) If you are able to use your class time to actually speak Persian, don't worry if you are only ever able to speak with other learners. Speaking with your fellow learners is a great way of improving your fluency because other learners will usually use words and elevations you understand; they will also usually speak quite slowly and carefully––unlike most native speakers! Second, use your grammar books to practise reading—so long as you remember not to get distracted by the complex descriptions of rules. Remember, it is not the rules that are necessarily complicated, it's how they are described that is complicated. In particular, don't be distracted by the grammatical labels used. The tendency to resort to arcane terminology is particularly common in grammar books of lesser-taught languages like Persian, which is ironic really because the need for simpler labels is all the more important! Just use your grammar books to practise your reading and to pick up new words and elevations. However, neither speaking Persian in class nor using your grammar books to practise your reading is what I mean by "doing things" in Persian; you should try as much as possible to do all the other things you do on a regular basis—work, watch TV, write emails, browse the Internet, play computer games, talk to your children, etc—in Persian.

Admittedly, doing all your everyday activities in Persian is easier if you live in a Persian-speaking environment, but there is absolutely no obstacle to doing so so long as you can access modern technology; if you have access to the Internet, you can practise Persian in a great deal of situations. Go on the Internet and watch free Persian movies or TV programmes. Read websites in Persian. Join online Persian chatrooms. Go on social networking sites to find a local Persian society or club and attend their events. Participate in a language exchange with Persian students at your local university (have an hour of conversation in English, followed by an hour in Persian, or otherwise help them with their English by proofreading their work). Make a prank phonecall to a swimming pool in Iran, asking about opening times! Switch the language of your web browser, phone, and favourite computer game to Persian (if possible). Order Persian books online (especially ones with translations in English) and cheap Iranian magazines and newspapers. For extra pronunciation practice, download a Persian song you like, learn it by heart, and sing it back to yourself as you play it in your car. If you want to know the meaning of a word but don't have a dictionary, type the word into a popular search engine but click on an image search instead of the usual text search; if lots of images of the same thing come back, chances are good that you've discovered the meaning of this word. If you don't know how to pronounce a word you encounter in Persian script (which will happen a lot), there are websites that list words in different languages, and you can click on these words to hear how they are pronounced. In short, if you have access to the Internet, there is no excuse for not "doing things" in Persian.

Should I record new rules, words, and elevations?

Traditionally, language learners have recorded lists of new words, for example in a notebook or word-processed document (as I have done in Chapter Three). If you do this, I suggest you use a word-processed document because you will then be able to go back and do such things as find words more easily, modify the text you have typed, rearrange lists of words to give yourself tests, add colour to divide words into categories or levels of difficulty, and go back and add associated words such as helpers. Colour is particularly useful for those languages that have different types (or "genders") of object and different ways of talking about more than one object for example. Typing all "feminine" objects in a red font, all "masculine" objects in blue, and all "neuter" objects in yellow is an obvious advantage (particularly for the visually minded), though for Persian of course, none of this is necessary. However, if you do keep lists of new words (or elevations or rules for that matter), there comes a point at which your lists become so huge that they are unmanageable. Languages are "information heavy"; essentially, knowledge of a language is a huge mass of information in your brain, and it soon becomes very inconvenient to externally record this information on paper or screen. For this reason, I would suggest that you still use the words, rules, and elevations as a starting point but after that, just record new information directly to the "notebook" of your own brain. If you think about it, unless you plan on writing the most comprehensive and definitive Persian dictionary or grammar book ever produced, you will have to do this at some point; you will never be able to write a note of absolutely every new word, rule, or elevation you will ever encounter in Persian—so you might as well start relying solely on your brain sooner rather than later.

Although it might sound counterintuitive, whether you adopt this approach or not, don't worry about forgetting information you have not written down. Being exposed to actual Persian is like doing a revision test on any artificial list of words, rules, or elevations you might otherwise produce—only better, because you'll be having an authentic conversation while you do so, be watching a movie and following its storyline, or be otherwise practising your language skills in a more natural context. Crucially, you will automatically be "revising" the language you actually need, namely the words, rules, and elevations that occur in the types of conversations you actually have and in the types of texts you actually read. That annoying little word you haven't noted down is still part of the language, and it isn't going anywhere; you will encounter it again at some point. Of course, relying on your brain like this does lack the certainty of a written note, but your brain more than makes up for this by the sheer volume of information it can hold (and you can't accidentally leave your brain behind on the train...).

Isn't it wrong to translate new words into English?

In this book, English is used extensively as the "default" basis of comparison; features of Persian are described only in relation to English and not in relation to abstract grammatical concepts. Equally, the rules of Persian have been described only to the extent that they differ from English; for example, if the order of certain words in specific phrases is the same as in English, this rule has not been explicitly stated. Persian words have also been given a direct English translation; indeed, the whole notion of "elevations" is based on the existence of a literal translation (however strange) of any Persian phrase you encounter. Depending on your experience of language learning, this may be a new approach to you. Modern methods of language teaching tend not to rely so much on the learner's first language. For example, many language teachers believe that you should approach learning new words just as a child who is learning his or her first language does; the word "cat" for example, which is *"gorbe"* in Persian, should be approached not with the reasoning that "the word 'cat' is *'gorbe'* in Persian" but that "the small furry animal that chases mice is a *'gorbe'* when we're speaking Persian". In my opinion, this is a very effective method that may allow you to actually "think" in the language from the start—but only if you have the time and the resources (as children do) to wait for a cat to walk by or come up in conversation while your native-speaking friends are around, who comment on the *"gorbe"* and point to it, before you figure out the spelling of the word when you encounter it two years later in your schoolbook... If you spend 15 years in an Iranian school having lessons and playing games with your Persian-speaking friends, who speak no English, then this is a viable method.

If you have a busy job and little time (like most adults) and are too old to go back to school, then there is a very simple, effective, and alternative way of learning what the word *"gorbe"* means: just learn *"gorbe* – cat". If you do this, you know what the word *"gorbe"* means, how to pronounce it, how to spell it in Persian script (if you use the spelling system in this book), how to use it grammatically, and you can guess that it appears in much the same types of phrases as it does in English. Instead of avoiding English, I believe that you already have an amazing resource to help you learn any new language: your first language! This is a resource that will allow you to learn a lot of words, rules, and elevations much more easily and quickly than you would if you relied on abstract grammatical concepts such as "tenses" or "person" etc and tried to learn new information in Persian without resorting to direct translation. Of course, when you become more advanced in Persian and encounter the word *"gorbe"*, you will automatically think of that small furry animal that chases mice—but don't feel you need to do this when you first begin to learn the language.

I hope you have enjoyed learning Persian using this book,
and I hope you have found at least some of it useful.
Good luck in your language learning!

Index

Helpers

Pronunciation

Elevations

Persian script

Spoken and written Persian

Language learning

Traditional grammatical terms

27066854R00101

Printed in Great Britain
by Amazon